Study Guide

TO ACCOMPANY

Domosh/Neumann/Price/Jordan-Bychkov

THE HUMAN MOSAIC
A Cultural Approach to Human Geography

Twelfth Edition

Michael Andrew Kukral, Ph.D.
Associate Professor of Geography
Rose-Hulman Institute of Technology

W.H. Freeman and Company
New York

ISBN-13: 978-1-4292-5352-9
ISBN-10: 1-4292-5352-5

Printed in the United States of America

First printing

W. H. Freeman and Company
41 Madison Avenue
New York, NY 10010
Houndmills, Basingstoke RG21 6XS, England

CONTENTS

ACKNOWLEDGMENTS

Work experience and education have always been very important in my family. This brief guide is dedicated to the great teachers in my life: my parents. To the memory of my late father, Clarence Ferdinand Kukral, an upholsterer in Cleveland for sixty-two years, and to the memory of my mother, Ada Mae Kukral, a wonderful person from a farm in Bath, Ohio, who loved art, gardening, and people. Our house was always filled with interesting books and things and out the back door was, what seemed to me, endless woods to explore.

ABOUT THE AUTHOR

Dr. Michael Andrew Kukral is an associate professor of geography at Rose-Hulman Institute of Technology in Terre Haute, Indiana. He received his Ph.D. from the University of Kentucky and has been distinguished for excellent teaching at Ohio University, the University of Kentucky, and at Rose-Hulman Institute of Technology. Kukral previously earned a B.S., an M.A., and an M.Sc. from Ohio University in Athens.

Dr. Kukral was a Fulbright scholar in the Czech capital of Prague during the "Velvet Revolution" and is the author of the book *Prague 1989: Theater of Revolution, A Study in Humanistic Political Geography*, published by Columbia University Press. He has traveled extensively in continental Europe and has taught field study courses and led student travel programs there.

Since 1999, Professor Kukral has been the director of the geography program at Rose-Hulman Institute of Technology, one of our nation's top engineering, math, and science private colleges. In 2011, he developed a program for the Rose-Hulman Football Team to prepare them for travel-study to Prague and for a game against the Austrian national team in Vienna (Rose-Hulman won in overtime).

A native of the Cuyahoga Valley and a member of the Revere High School Hall of Fame, Mike Kukral is also a noted authority on the history, restoration, and music of the player piano. He enjoys spending time at his cabin in coastal Oregon and likes hiking, camping, cooking, music, backpacking, and being with his family and grey cats Kitty, Oliver, and Cairo.

CHAPTER 1

HUMAN GEOGRAPHY: A CULTURAL APPROACH

Extended Chapter Outline (Including Key Terms)

I. Definition and historic development of geography
   A. The growth and development of geography
   B. What is human geography?

II. What is a cultural approach to human geography?
   A. Learned collective behavior
   B. Spatial variation and spatial pattern
   C. Physical environments
   D. The example of wheat cultivation
   E. Spatial models

III. The region
   A. Definition of region
      1. Formal regions: core-periphery patterns
      2. Functional regions: Nodes
      3. Vernacular culture regions: A perceived region

IV. Mobility
   A. Diffusion: Spatial spread of learned ideas
   B. Independent invention
   C. Expansion diffusion and relocation diffusion: stimulus, hierarchical, and contagious diffusion
   D. Time-distance decay: absorbing and permeable barriers
   E. Migration

V. Globalization
   A. Definition
   B. Uneven development

VI. Nature-Culture
   A. Cultural ecology
   B. Environmental determinism
   C. Possibilism
   D. Environmental perception: natural hazards
   E. Humans as modifiers of the Earth: ecofeminism

VII. Cultural landscape
   A. Definition
   B. Global climate change
   C. Symbolic landscapes
   D. Three principal aspects of cultural landscape

LEARNING OBJECTIVES

After reading this chapter *and* studying the maps and illustrations, you should be able to:

1. Briefly trace the historical development of geography.

2. Define *geography* and how geographers approach the study of Earth and its people.

3. Grasp the meaning of human geography and understand its basic topics, themes, and areas of study.

4. Describe, outline, compare, and give examples from the five major themes of cultural geography: region, mobility, globalization, nature-culture, and cultural landscape.

5. Begin to use the Internet and maps as essential tools of your education and understanding of the world.

FIGURE 1.13. Chongqing and San Francisco

1. Explain the contrasting appearance of street patterns on both maps.

_____

_____

_____

2. Are either of these street patterns a good case for environmental determinism? Why or why not?

_____

_____

_____

3. Which street system is more practical? Explain.

_____

_____

_____

7. Formal regions in geography often display a core-periphery pattern.
    a. true
    b. false

8. Cultural homogeneity is the hallmark of a:
    a. functional culture region
    b. formal culture region
    c. vernacular culture region
    d. multiple-trait area
    e. none of the above

9. Mona Domosh's "Notebook" entry looks at:
    a. current globalization in Russia
    b. the fall of the Soviet Union
    c. early-twentieth-century globalization in Russia
    d. economics in the new Russia
    e. both a and c

10. Globalization is a process that really took off in the _____ century.
    a. sixteenth
    b. seventeenth
    c. eighteenth
    d. nineteenth
    e. twentieth

11. Uneven development basically refers to:
    a. the HDI only
    b. the HDI and GDP
    c. distribution of resources
    d. location of countries
    e. cultural ecology

12. Nodes, or central points where activities are coordinated and directed, are a common characteristic of a:
    a. functional culture region
    b. formal culture region
    c. vernacular culture region
    d. multiple-trait area
    e. none of the above

13. Clearly defined borders are a common feature of a:
    a. functional region
    b. formal region
    c. vernacular culture region
    d. multiple-trait area
    e. none of the above

14. Which of the following is NOT an example of a functional region?
    a. coal fields of northern Appalachia
    b. newspaper circulation area
    c. Korean-language area
    d. Cleveland metropolitan area
    e. the state of Laos

15. A vernacular region is often considered to be a region:
    a. clearly demarcated on a map
    b. with strong functional and formal features
    c. perceived to exist by its inhabitants
    d. with traditional structural traits
    e. none of the above

16. The late Denis Gosgrove was an important:
    a. behavioral geographer
    b. designer of spatial models
    c. contributor to African urban studies
    d. ecologist and climatologist
    e. cultural geographer

17. Most geographical studies of the cultural landscape have focused on three principal aspects:
    land-division patterns, architecture, and _____.
    a. barn types
    b. settlement forms
    c. ethnicity
    d. food and drink
    e. spatial-temporal patterns of transportation

18. The wavelike spread of ideas primarily involves the concept of:
    a. stimulus diffusion
    b. hierarchical diffusion
    c. contagious diffusion
    d. absorbing barriers
    e. none of the above

19. The study of the interaction between culture and environment is termed:
    a. cultural ecology
    b. neighborhood effect
    c. environmental science
    d. humanistic geography
    e. biogeography

20. Environmental determinism was a common doctrine of belief among geographers during the:
    a. mid-nineteenth century
    b. 1950s and 1960s
    c. late eighteenth century
    d. early twentieth century
    e. 1970s

21. The belief that cultural heritage is at least as important as the physical environment in affecting human behavior is usually associated with:
    a. environmental determinism
    b. possibilism
    c. two-trait regions
    d. single-trait regions
    e. material landscape

22. The theme of cultural integration, if improperly used, can lead the geographer to:
    a. social science
    b. preadaptive behavior
    c. cultural determinism
    d. geomancy
    e. possibilism

23. Model building, theory, and space are terms and devices usually associated with the _____ approach in cultural geography.
    a. humanistic
    b. humans-as-modifiers-of-the-Earth
    c. cultural ecological
    d. landscape interpretation
    e. social science

24. Place, topophilia, sense of place, and subjectivity are terms and ideas usually associated with the _____ approach in cultural geography.
    a. humanistic
    b. humans-as-modifiers-of-the-Earth
    c. cultural ecological
    d. landscape interpretation
    e. social science

25. The Eiffel Tower in Paris is part of the city skyline. This is an example of a(n):
    a. artistic landscape
    b. architectural landscape
    c. symbolic landscape
    d. transnational urban core
    e. global heritage site

PART TWO: Short-answer and fill-in-the-blank (probable essay-type questions)

26. The authors of the textbook are: _____

27. Human geography is the study of:

    _____
    _____
    _____

15

28. The cultural approach in human geography is:

_____

_____

_____

29. The five themes in human geography are:
   a. _____
   b. _____
   c. _____
   d. _____
   e. _____

30. Define culture.

_____

_____

_____

31. Explain the difference between formal regions and functional regions.

_____

_____

_____

_____

32. Give an example of a core-periphery pattern.

_____

_____

_____

33. What is globalization?

_____

_____

_____

_____

34. Explain why the German-language region is different from the country of Germany in the perspective of human geography.

_____

_____

_____

35. How are vernacular culture regions different from formal and functional regions?

_____

_____

36. Explain the difference between hierarchical diffusion and stimulus diffusion:

_____

_____

_____

37. What is meant by time-distance decay?

38. Explain the difference between environmental determinism, cultural ecology, and possibilism.

39. What is humanistic geography?

40. Examples of natural hazards are:

41. What role does "perception" play in studies of human geography?

42. Describe the theme of cultural integration.

43. Explain the difference between the geographic concepts of "space" and "place."

44. List some actual examples of the cultural landscape known to you.

CHAPTER TWO

MANY WORLDS: GEOGRAPHIES OF CULTURAL DIFFERENCE

Extended Chapter Outline (Including Key Terms)

I. Geographies of Cultural Difference
    A. Many cultures
    B. Classifying cultures

II. Regions of Difference
    A. Material folk culture regions
    B. Popular culture regions
        1. Placelessness
        2. Music, food, and drink
    C. Indigenous culture
    D. Vernacular culture regions

III. Mobility
    A. Diffusion in popular culture
    B. Advertising
    C. Communications barriers
    D. Diffusion of the rodeo
    E. Blowguns

IV. Globalization
    A. Difference to convergence
    B. Consumption
    C. Place images

V. Nature-Culture
    A. Indigenous ecology
    B. Global economy
    C. Folk ecology
    D. Gendered nature
    E. Nature in popular culture

VI. Cultural Landscape
    A. Folk architecture
    B. Folk housing in North America
    C. Folk housing in Africa south of the Sahara
    D. Landscapes of popular culture
    E. Leisure landscapes
    F. Elitist landscapes
    G. The American scene

VII. Conclusion
    A. Doing geography
    B. The Internet and other sources

LEARNING OBJECTIVES

After reading this chapter *and* studying the maps and illustrations, you should be able to:

1. Define, identify, and describe indigenous, folk, and popular cultures and their respective regions and landscapes.

2. Understand and explain various examples of folk and popular culture diffusion.

3. Describe the relationship between nature and indigenous, folk, and popular cultures.

4. Provide examples and explain how globalization integrates various cultural practices.

5. Discuss how the cultural landscape is shaped and affected by folk and popular cultures.

6. Recognize the role of globalization and folk and popular culture in your own family, region, or heritage.

SELECTED MAP READING AND INTERPRETATION

This section of the study guide is intended to increase your map-reading and interpretation skills. It will also help you apply the text readings to visual and spatial displays of concepts, themes, and examples in human and cultural geography.

A world atlas (in print or online) will be very useful in completing this section of the study guide and will enhance your comprehension of the maps in the textbook. Ask your instructor to recommend an appropriate web site or atlas to purchase (or visit the map collection at your library). A world atlas is essential for your personal reference library, not only during this course, but throughout your college career.

After reading the text and studying the related map and its captions, answer the following questions.

FIGURE 2.1. Folk cultural survival regions of the United States and southern Canada

1. Identify the folk culture of your local region. Can you think of any examples of existing material folk culture or former evidence of material folk culture?

   _____

   _____

   _____

2. From north to south, what are the folk culture regions of the Rocky Mountains?

   _____

   _____

   _____

3. What are the two locations of Acadian French folk culture? What is another name used for this culture in some locales?

   _____

   _____

   _____

FIGURE 2.8. Three examples of the 40 lifestyle clusters in U.S. popular culture

1. How were the data collected for the creation of this map?

   _____

   _____

   _____

2. What are the definitions of "Gray Power," "Old Yankee Rows," and "Norma Rae–ville"?

   _____

   _____

   _____

3. How do you see this map changing during the next 20 years? Has it changed already?

_____
_____
_____

FIGURE 2.9. *Fast-food sales as a share of total restaurant sales, by state, 1997*

1. What might account for the spatial variation in this aspect of popular culture?

_____
_____
_____

2. Does this pattern bear any similarity to the map of traditional and folk cultures shown in Figure 2.1?

_____
_____
_____

3. What does this suggest about the convergence hypothesis, which holds that regional cultures in America are collapsing into a national or global culture?

_____
_____
_____

FIGURE 2.14. *The Mayan culture region in Middle America*

1. Identify Mayan culture regions. Do you see any relationship to contemporary international boundaries? How were the modern state boundaries created?

_____
_____
_____

2. Using an atlas, identify the climate and vegetation located in Mayan culture regions. Are they different from those in other areas on this map? Did the Mayans thrive in specific environments? Why or why not?

_____
_____
_____

3. Look at the location of Mayan cities. Can you identify any patterns of settlement or site selection for these cities? Based on their urban locations, would you say the Mayans were an interior- or coastal-oriented society? Explain the differences.

_____
_____
_____

FIGURE 2.15. The indigenous culture region of the Andes

1. Identify the area of the Inca Empire. Which countries are located there today? Do you see any boundaries of the Inca Empire that correspond with contemporary international boundaries?

_____

_____

_____

2. The topography of the Incan culture regions shows high relief. Using an atlas, identify the various elevation changes where Inca culture exists. Would you describe the Inca as a mountain culture? What does the term "mountain culture" mean?

_____

_____

_____

3. Can you think of any reasons why the Incans didn't settle and develop the coastal areas? What environmental challenges exist in this coastal region of South America?

_____

_____

_____

FIGURE 2.17. The vernacular Middle West or Midwest

1. What might account for the differences between this map and Figure 2.16?

_____

_____

_____

2. Why would some respondents (less than 10 percent) claim to live in the Midwest in states such as Florida, California, and New Hampshire?

_____

_____

_____

3. Which states on this map, such as Ohio, can be considered on the Midwest periphery? Why?

_____

_____

_____

FIGURE 2.20. Former distribution of the blowgun

1. Were the two widely separated areas of blowgun use the result of independent invention or cultural diffusion?

_____

_____

2. Compare and contrast blowgun occurrence in the Indian and Pacific ocean countries to the distribution of the Austronesian languages on the map in Chapter 4.

_____
_____
_____

3. Can you think of any reasons for the lack of blowgun use in continental Africa, Australia, or southern South America?

_____
_____
_____

FIGURE 2.22. Global congruence of cultural and biological diversity

1. Areas of concentrations are mainly located in tropical zones on Earth. Explain why both biodiversity and cultural diversity clusters are in the regions that straddle the equator.

_____
_____
_____

2. Name at least five countries that have a high concentration of biodiversity and indigenous peoples.

_____
_____
_____

3. What may account for low biodiversity in places such as Australia, Algeria, Somalia, and Saudi Arabia?

_____
_____
_____

18. vernacular culture and vernacular regions

_____
_____
_____

19. convergence

_____
_____
_____

20. reverse hierarchical diffusion

_____
_____
_____

21. rodeo

_____
_____
_____

22. international diffusion

_____
_____
_____

23. geography of consumption

_____
_____
_____

24. the convergence hypothesis

_____
_____
_____

25. mapping personal preference

_____
_____
_____

26. place image

_____
_____
_____

27. elitist landscape

_____
_____

28. gentleman farm

_____
_____
_____

29. landscape of consumption

_____
_____
_____

30. landscape of leisure

_____
_____
_____

31. the "American scene"

_____
_____
_____

32. residential front yards

_____
_____
_____

33. sense of place

_____
_____
_____

34. fast-food regions

_____
_____
_____

35. the vernacular "Midwest"

_____
_____
_____

36. folk and popular architecture

_____
_____
_____

37. New England "large"

_____
_____

38. "upright and wing"

_____
_____
_____

39. "saddlebag" house

_____
_____
_____

40. "shotgun" house

_____
_____
_____

41. "Ontario" farmhouse

_____
_____
_____

42. What is "Rod's Notebook" about? What do you think about this topic?

_____
_____
_____

REVIEW: Self-Evaluation Tests

PART ONE: Multiple-choice

Circle the best answer for each question. When you are finished, read each question again with your selected answer. After you are satisfied with your practice test, use the answer key in the back of the study guide to check your responses.

1. The best active example of a folk culture in the United States is the:
   a. Hispanic culture of the Southwest
   b. Cuban culture in Florida
   c. Amish culture in Ohio and Pennsylvania
   d. African-American culture in the Lower South
   e. family farm of the Midwest

2. Food, tools, furniture, buildings, and clothing are all considered:
   a. material culture
   b. folklore
   c. living history
   d. folk geography
   e. none of the above

3. Folk dialects, religions, and worldviews can be regarded as:
   a. traditional lifestyles
   b. popular culture
   c. cultural artifacts
   d. nonmaterial culture
   e. none of the above

4. Active folk cultures would most likely be found in:
   a. North America
   b. Equatorial Africa
   c. Japan and Taiwan
   d. Scandinavia, especially Iceland
   e. the Middle East

5. Perhaps the most enduring feature of folk culture is:
   a. architecture
   b. language
   c. clothing
   d. occupation
   e. food

6. Folk culture spreads by the same processes of diffusion as do other elements and types of culture, but more rapidly.
   a. true
   b. false

7. Detailed knowledge about the environment by many traditional cultures is often termed:
   a. cultural convergence
   b. agricultural adaptation
   c. indigenous technical knowledge
   d. knowledge of ecological awareness
   e. deep ecology

8. If one or more nonfunctional features of blowguns occurred in both South America and Indonesia, then it is logical to surmise that the distribution of blowguns:
   a. is based on the theory of independent invention
   b. is independent of functionality
   c. is a result of diffusion
   d. occurred after the year 1492
   e. none of the above

9. In southern Africa, this term often refers to a group or compound of buildings:
   a. kraal
   b. ndebele
   c. hausa
   d. transvaal
   e. station

10. In the Mexican folk culture region along the southern border of Texas, folk medicine is still widely practiced by:
    a. curanderos
    b. shamans
    c. faith healers
    d. witch doctors
    e. caballeros

11. Moonshine corn whiskey has been associated with the folk culture of the _____ since the 1700s.
    a. Upper Midwest
    b. Gulf Coast
    c. Rocky Mountains
    d. Great Lakes
    e. Upland South

12. Country and western music in the United States has its origins in the folk culture of the:
    a. Upper Midwest
    b. Gulf Coast
    c. Rocky Mountains
    d. Great Lakes
    e. Upland South

13. A spatial standardization that diminishes cultural variety and demeans the human spirit can result in:
    a. place image
    b. nonplace image

c. placelessness

d. aspatial values

e. popular culture

14. According to the text, the leading region or places for beer consumption in the United States is (are):

a. the Lower South

b. the Upper Midwest

c. California and Florida

d. the Northeast

e. the Southwest

15. Nearly all professional sports in the United States were first organized in the:

a. 1920s

b. 1950s

c. 1930s

d. 1890s

e. nineteenth century

16. Regions perceived to exist by their inhabitants are termed:

a. popular regions

b. vernacular regions

c. folk regions

d. perceived regions

e. psychological regions

17. Resentment toward imported goods can be termed:

a. racist

b. consumer nationalism

c. postconsumption culture

d. antiglobalization

e. material xenophobia

18. Time-distance decay in popular culture diffusion is _____ folk culture.

a. stronger than

b. considerably stronger than

c. weaker than

d. considerably weaker than

e. about the same as

19. Popular culture is considered to have a _____ rate of diffusion.

a. slow

b. average

c. rapid

d. lateral

e. dynamic

20. The rodeo, as an example of popular culture diffusion, has its origins in:
    a. Spanish settlement areas
    b. primarily Texas
    c. Montana and Oklahoma
    d. southern California
    e. both b and c

21. Diaspora communities are made up of primarily:
    a. French, British, or Spanish colonists
    b. Jewish groups fleeing oppression
    c. former political refugees
    d. Africans and South Asians
    e. immigrants

22. Of the following European countries, which probably do not participate much in Western popular culture?
    a. Czech Republic, Lithuania, and Austria
    b. Switzerland, France, and Luxembourg
    c. Norway, Finland, and Estonia
    d. Germany, Poland, and Belgium
    e. none of the above

23. Popular culture, by definition, does not display regionalization.
    a. true
    b. false

24. The devices of diffusion in popular culture require large amounts of electricity and fossil fuels.
    a. true
    b. false

25. Popular culture makes exceedingly high demands on:
    a. national parks
    b. wilderness areas
    c. coastal zones
    d. national recreation areas
    e. all of the above

26. Many social scientists assume that the results of causal forces in popular culture would be to homogenize culture. This view is called:
    a. placelessness
    b. the time-distance continuum
    c. clustering
    d. the convergence hypothesis
    e. none of the above

27. Photography, literature, television, and film often contribute to the creation of:
    a. peripheral place zones
    b. tourist illiteracy

c. place image
d. the modernity hypothesis
e. none of the above

28. Which of the following would probably be labeled as a gentleman farm?
    a. sheep ranching for wool production
    b. horticulture of nuts and fruits
    c. fish farming in the Mississippi
    d. thoroughbred horse breeding in Kentucky
    e. organic farming

29. In stage 5 of Jakle and Mattson's model of commercial strip evolution, the:
    a. residential function disappears
    b. commercial function dominates
    c. gas stations are introduced
    d. single-family residence dominates
    e. none of the above

30. The most reflective landscape of consumption in popular culture is (are) the:
    a. commercial strip
    b. shopping mall
    c. central business district (CBD)
    d. gentleman farm
    e. hotel and convention complexes

31. Lowenthal concludes that the preeminence of _____ is an important part of the "American scene."
    a. the cult of bigness
    b. ugliness
    c. big hair and TV talk shows
    d. function over form
    e. manicured front lawns

32. Bluegrass music has its beginnings in several states in the United States, but derives its name from the state of:
    a. Texas
    b. Kentucky
    c. Virginia
    d. West Virginia
    e. Tennessee

33. Stones are often used as the traditional building material of the farmers of:
    a. Northern Europe
    b. Russia
    c. Canada
    d. the Mediterranean
    e. Southeast Asia

34. The Ndebele house ornamentation is a good indicator of traditional:
    a. stone construction
    b. half-timbering
    c. communal housing
    d. cultural identity
    e. unit farmstead

35. An example of an African-American folk dwelling is the:
    a. shotgun house
    b. New England large
    c. upright and wing
    d. traditional Georgian
    e. saddlebag house

36. As Yankee folk migrated westward, they developed this type of house:
    a. shotgun
    b. New England large
    c. upright and wing
    d. traditional Georgian
    e. saddlebag

PART TWO: Short-answer (probable essay-type questions)

37. In which major world regions are active folk cultures most likely to be found?

38. Provide some examples of both material and nonmaterial culture.

39. Briefly describe the difference between indigenous and folk culture.

40. List some of the defining elements of popular culture.

41. Provide an example and define "placelessness."

42. What is the role of popular music in the geography of popular culture?

_____

_____

_____

43. Discuss the regional variation of rodeos in the United States.

_____

_____

_____

44. What is a vernacular culture region and how does it apply to popular culture?

_____

_____

_____

45. Discuss the role of advertising in the process of diffusion.

_____

_____

_____

46. What are some barriers to the diffusion of popular culture?

_____

_____

_____

47. What are elements of Mayan and Incan culture?

_____

_____

_____

48. What are some of the environmental influences on popular culture?

_____

_____

_____

49. State some specific examples of popular culture's impact on the environment.

_____

_____

_____

50. Explain the convergence hypothesis. Do you agree with it?

_____

_____

_____

51. What is a place image and how are place images created?

_____

_____

_____

52. Provide some characteristics of an elitist landscape.

_____

_____

_____

53. What is a landscape of consumption?

_____

_____

_____

54. Provide a definition and example of a leisure landscape.

_____

_____

_____

55. Explain the meaning of Lowenthal's "American scene."

_____

_____

_____

56. What are some examples of popular culture in your home area?

_____

_____

_____

57. Why do you think American pop culture has become an international phenomenon?

_____

_____

_____

58. As North Americans, what features of other countries' popular culture do we absorb?

_____

_____

_____

59. What are some of the traditional folk culture regions of the western United States?

_____

_____

_____

60. Discuss some culture elements and provide an example of a folk food region.

_____

_____

_____

61. Use folk songs to demonstrate the process of folk cultural diffusion.

_____

_____

62. Briefly explain the two conflicting ideas or theories concerning the global distribution of the blowgun.

_____

_____

_____

63. What are reasons behind the cultural practice of "gentlemen farms"?

_____

_____

_____

64. What are three major contributions to the folk geography of the United States attributed to the Upland South region?

_____

_____

_____

65. Describe the theme of globalization with regard to the exchange between popular and folk culture.

_____

_____

_____

66. Select an area of the world outside of North America and describe the traditional building materials and their relationship to the natural environment.

_____

_____

_____

CHAPTER THREE

POPULATION GEOGRAPHY: SHAPING THE HUMAN MOSAIC

Extended Chapter Outline (Including Key Terms)

I. Demographic Regions
   A. Population distribution and density
      1. Population density
      2. Thickly, moderately, and thinly settled areas
      3. Carrying capacity
   B. Patterns of natality
      1. Birthrates
      2. Fertility rates
   C. Death rates
   D. Demographic transition
   E. Age distributions
   F. Geography of gender
      1. Sex ratio
      2. Gender roles
   H. Standard of living

II. Mobility in Population Geography
   A. Migration
      1. Kennewick Man
      2. Push-and-pull factors
   B. Diseases on the move: example of HIV/AIDS

III. Population Globalization
   A. The population explosion
      1. Crucial elements
      2. Malthusian
      3. Neo-Malthusian
   B. The Rule of 72
   C. Population control programs

IV. Nature-Culture
   A. Environmental influence
      1. Climatic factors
      2. Coastal locations
   B. Environmental perception and population distribution
   C. Population density and environmental alteration

V. The Cultural Landscape
 A. Farm villages
  1. Farmsteads and clustered settlements
  2. Environmental determinants
 B. Isolated farmsteads
 C. Historical factors
 D. Political and economic factors
  1. Ethnic cleansing
  2. Nation-states
 E. Depopulation
 F. Seeing geography: Kolkata, India

VI. Conclusions

LEARNING OBJECTIVES

After reading this chapter *and* studying the maps and illustrations, you should be able to:

1. Understand the terms and concepts used by geographers to study the human population.

2. Give examples of the various factors influencing human migration and population mobility.

3. Distinguish and discuss the differences among population distribution, population density, and population composition.

4. Show the relationship between population and nature-culture, including factors of human perception and gender.

5. Understand the role of political, economic, and especially cultural phenomena in influencing the human population.

6. Distinguish various settlement patterns and farm village patterns.

7. Continue to improve your ability to read and interpret the cultural landscape.

SELECTED MAP READING AND INTERPRETATION

This section of the Study Guide is intended to increase your map-reading and interpretation skills. It will also help you apply the text readings to visual and spatial displays of concepts, themes, and examples in human and cultural geography.

A world atlas (in print or online) will be very useful in completing this section of the Study Guide and will enhance your comprehension of the maps in the textbook. Ask your instructor to recommend an appropriate web site or atlas to purchase (or visit the map collection at your library). A world atlas is essential for your personal reference library, not only during this course, but throughout your college career.

After reading the text and studying the related map and its captions, answer the following questions.

FIGURE 3.1. Population density in the world

1. It is well known that China has the largest population in the world. The pattern of population distribution in China, however, shows a clear east-west division. Can you think of any environmental or economic factors influencing this pattern in China? Do you see a similar distribution pattern in the United States, Brazil, and Australia? Provide a few statements to support your answer.

    _____
    _____
    _____

2. Is it reasonable to state that population density is usually highest in coastal regions? Select a few specific countries or regions to support your answer.

    _____
    _____
    _____

3. What is the pattern of population density in the tropics? Use the continents of Africa, Asia, and South America in your answer.

    _____
    _____
    _____

4. Can you think of any reasons for the band of high population density running across the interior of Central Europe?

    _____
    _____
    _____

FIGURE 3.4. The total fertility rate (TFR) in the world

1. Which regions of the world have the highest TFR?

   _____
   _____
   _____

2. Can you think of any reasons why some Latin American countries, such as Honduras, have higher TFR than others?

   _____
   _____
   _____

3. Compare the data on this map with the data shown in Figure 3.1. Does this comparison illustrate that the population of China and India must be declining? Why or why not?

   _____
   _____
   _____

FIGURE 3.6. The geography of HIV/AIDS

1. What is the population density of the countries with the highest rate of HIV/AIDS?

   _____
   _____
   _____

2. Where is the rate of HIV/AIDS lowest, according to this map? Can you make some hypotheses about the reasons for the low numbers? What role does government have in reporting these numbers?

   _____
   _____
   _____

3. Can you find a relationship between HIV/AIDS and the economy of a region or country? Any examples?

   _____
   _____
   _____

FIGURE 3.9. Geography of contraception in the modern world

1. Where do the highest percentages of contraception usage occur? Are these rich or poor areas?

   _____
   _____
   _____

2. The white areas on this map are an indication of what?

_____

_____

_____

3. Compare this map with Figure 3.3. What can you interpret from this comparison?

_____

_____

_____

FIGURE 3.10. The world pattern of youth and old age

1. Do these maps show a relationship between economy and age? Why or why not? Compare Europe and Africa.

_____

_____

_____

2. What probably accounts for the older populations living in West Virginia, Florida, and Pennsylvania? Explain.

_____

_____

_____

3. Can you think of any cultural or environmental reasons for the patterns on these maps?

_____

_____

_____

FIGURE 3.16. The present world pattern of infant mortality rates

1. The highest infant mortality rates are found in which countries? What do you believe are the reasons for this?

_____

_____

_____

2. Can you detect any geographic or regional patterns in Africa for infant mortality rates? Explain.

_____

_____

_____

3. Other than poverty and education, what factors do you think influence infant mortality rates?

_____

_____

_____

CREATE YOUR PERSONAL GLOSSARY OF KEY TERMS, PEOPLE, AND PLACES

In the space below, write a definition and provide an example of each key term that is sufficient for **your understanding**. It is an excellent study habit to organize your response in three parts:

1. A formal definition or identification from the textbook

2. A definition of the key term in **your own words**

3. An example to increase your understanding of the key term

KEY TERMS, PEOPLE, AND PLACES

1. geodemography

_____
_____
_____

2. population density

_____
_____
_____

3. demographic regions

_____
_____
_____

4. population distribution

_____
_____
_____

5. thickly, moderately, and thinly settled areas

_____
_____
_____

6. carrying capacity

_____
_____
_____

7. natality

_____
_____
_____

8. birthrates

_____
_____
_____

9. fertility rate

_____
_____
_____

10. mortality

_____
_____
_____

11. death rates

_____
_____
_____

12. population explosion

_____
_____
_____

13. zero population growth

_____
_____
_____

14. TFR

_____
_____
_____

15. demographic transition

_____
_____
_____

16. Eurocentric

_____
_____
_____

17. population pyramid

_____

_____

_____

18. sex ratio

_____

_____

_____

19. gender roles

_____

_____

_____

20. migration

_____

_____

_____

21. voluntary and forced migration

_____

_____

_____

22. push-and-pull factors

_____

_____

_____

23. disease diffusion

_____

_____

_____

24. AIDS, HIV-1, HIV-2

_____

_____

_____

25. Rule of 72

_____

_____

_____

26. Malthusian

_____

_____

27. ethnic cleansing

28. interregional migration

29. Kennewick Man

30. personal space

31. settlement landscape

32. clustered settlements

33. farm villages

34. street village

35. green village

36. strong-point and wet-point settlements

_____
_____
_____

37. isolated farmsteads

_____
_____
_____

38. semiclustered rural settlement

_____
_____
_____

39. hamlet

_____
_____
_____

40. loose irregular and row villages

_____
_____
_____

41. Spanish-influenced architecture

_____
_____
_____

42. cenote

_____
_____
_____

43. Malthusian theory

_____
_____
_____

44. population geography

_____
_____
_____

45. depopulation

_____

_____

_____

REVIEW: Self-Evaluation Tests

PART ONE: Multiple-choice

Circle the best answer for each question. When you are finished, read each question again with your selected answer. After you are satisfied with your practice test, use the Answer Key in the back of the Study Guide to check your responses.

1. The current population of Earth is about:
    a. 2.9 billion
    b. 9.9 billion
    c. 4.5 billion
    d. 12 billion
    e. 6.8 billion

2. Population geographers primarily study the _____ aspects of demography.
    a. physical
    b. physiological
    c. ecological
    d. cultural
    e. distributive

3. The five most populous countries are Brazil, United States, China, India, and:
    a. Russia
    b. Indonesia
    c. Nigeria
    d. Germany
    e. Pakistan

4. Less than 5 percent of the world's population lives in the United States.
    a. true
    b. false

5. "Moderately settled areas" have about _____ persons per square mile.
    a. 500–700
    b. 250–500
    c. 60–250
    d. 2–60
    e. none of the above

6. The density beyond which people cease to be nutritionally self-sufficient is said to be above:
    a. carrying capacity
    b. physiological nutrition
    c. zero growth
    d. biological density
    e. caloric regression

7. Birth and death rates are measured in number per:
   a. hundred
   b. thousand
   c. hundred thousand
   d. million
   e. square mile

8. The three main population clusters of the world are eastern Asia, the Indian subcontinent, and:
   a. Europe
   b. China
   c. the eastern United States
   d. West Africa
   e. East Africa

9. At present rates, about how many years will it take for the world population to double?
   a. 15
   b. 20
   c. 30
   d. 40
   e. 50

10. The American tropics, North Africa, the Middle East, and Central Asia all have _____ death rates.
   a. very high
   b. high
   c. low
   d. average
   e. very low

11. Rapid population growth among humans began around the year:
   a. 1450
   b. 1930
   c. 1890
   d. 1820
   e. 1700

12. Malthus stated that famine and _____ would be constant checks of population growth.
   a. natural disasters
   b. poverty
   c. disease
   d. war
   e. accidents

13. In preindustrial societies, birth and death rates are both normally:
   a. high
   b. low
   c. moderate

d. very low

e. none of the above

14. Recently settled areas typically have more males than females.
    a. true
    b. false

15. Living in a farm village places the family on their agricultural land.
    a. true
    b. false

16. The most common type of migration is:
    a. forced
    b. push-and-pull
    c. international
    d. war refugee
    e. voluntary

17. The largest migration in history took place in the _____ century, when more than 50 million people left Europe.
    a. twentieth
    b. nineteenth
    c. eighteenth
    d. seventeenth
    e. sixteenth

18. In Africa, AIDS is a disease primarily affecting the _____ community.
    a. elderly
    b. upper economic social classes of a
    c. heterosexual
    d. homosexual
    e. Islamic

19. Areas of extremely high heat or cold are considered to be _____ climates, from the perspective of humans.
    a. "golden mean"
    b. wonderful
    c. defective
    d. marginal
    e. uninhabitable

20. Americans' usage accounts for about _____ percent of the world's resources consumed each year.
    a. 5
    b. 10
    c. 15
    d. 20
    e. 40

21. Farm villages are common throughout much of the rural American Midwest.
    a. true
    b. false

22. The "street village" is particularly common to:
    a. China
    b. Russia
    c. Latin America
    d. East Africa
    e. Southeast Asia

23. Dr. John Snow is famous for his understanding of:
    a. epidemiology
    b. cholera
    c. Bogota rising
    d. rural depopulation
    e. oil and population capacity

PART TWO: Short-answer (probable essay-type questions)

24. What do population geographers study, and what topics and processes are included in these studies?

    _____

    _____

    _____

25. Explain the difference between population distribution and population density.

    _____

    _____

    _____

26. What is the "Rule of 72"?

    _____

    _____

    _____

27. How is the fertility rate measured and what can this statistic indicate with regard to population patterns?

    _____

    _____

    _____

28. What is meant by "population explosion," and how and why did this event come about?

    _____

    _____

    _____

29. What are the contributions of Thomas Malthus to demographic studies? Are his ideas valid today?

_____

_____

_____

30. Briefly define and categorize the demographic transformation.

_____

_____

_____

31. What are population pyramids and what are the important contributions they provide to demographers?

_____

_____

_____

32. Describe several important push-and-pull factors of migration.

_____

_____

_____

33. Provide several examples of forced migration.

_____

_____

_____

34. Briefly describe the diffusion theory of AIDS.

_____

_____

_____

35. Define "Eurocentric."

_____

_____

_____

36. Give some examples of the environmental influence on population.

_____

_____

_____

37. How does human perception play a role in distribution and settlement patterns?

_____

_____

_____

LEARNING OBJECTIVES

After reading this chapter *and* studying the maps and illustrations, you should be able to:

1. Explain and understand the difference between a language family, a language, a dialect, and a linguistic accent.

2. Describe the diffusion process of several major language families throughout the world.

3. Demonstrate the various relationships between language and the natural environment.

4. Discuss the influence of nature and cultural environment on languages.

5. Explain the roles of cultural mobility and globalization in language patterns.

6. Understand the roles of language and religion in language patterns.

7. Interpret the cultural landscape by reading various toponyms.

8. Have a better understanding of the place or region where you live through interpreting local toponyms.

SELECTED MAP READING AND INTERPRETATION

This section of the Study Guide is intended to increase your map-reading and interpretation skills. It will also help you apply the text readings to visual and spatial displays of concepts, themes, and examples in human and cultural geography.

A world atlas (in print or online) will be very useful in completing this section of the Study Guide and will enhance your comprehension of the maps in the textbook. Ask your instructor to recommend an appropriate web site or atlas to purchase (or visit the map collection at your library). A world atlas is essential for your personal reference library, not only during this course, but throughout your college career.

After reading the text and studying the related map and its captions, answer the following questions.

FIGURE 4.2. Naming place is closely related to claiming place

1. Which countries' territorial claims overlap on this map? How does this affect place names?

    _____
    _____
    _____

2. State some specific examples of English, Norwegian, and Spanish words or connections on the landscape of Antarctica and match the country claims with the respective languages.

    _____
    _____
    _____

3. Conduct an Internet search for several of the places named after people. What do you find that is relevant to the map?

    _____
    _____
    _____

4. What are the names of each of the oceans that border Antarctica?

    _____
    _____
    _____

FIGURE 4.3. Major linguistic formal culture regions of the world

1. What is the most widespread or spatially dominant language subgroup spoken on each continent? (It is important to know the boundary between Asia and Europe!)

    _____

    _____

    _____

2. List five countries, including an African island state, where the Austronesian language subgroup is spoken.

    _____

    _____

    _____

3. Looking at this map, do you see the reason behind the name "Indo-European" family? Explain.

    _____

    _____

    _____

4. Identify the language subgroup for the following independent countries: Vietnam, South Korea, Cameroon, Eritrea, Suriname, Hungary, Iceland, and Lebanon.

    _____

    _____

    _____

FIGURE 4.7. Origin and diffusion of four major language families in the Eastern Hemisphere

1. What present-day countries comprise the source area, or hearth, of the Niger-Congo language family?

    _____

    _____

    _____

2. Where is the original source area of modern English?

    _____

    _____

    _____

FIGURE 4.10. Major dialects of North American English

1. What and where are the Missouri Apex and the Hoosier Apex?

    _____
    _____
    _____

2. Which dialects are spoken in Southern California, Kentucky, North Dakota, and most of Ohio? What do you think about this map? Is it correct, in your opinion? Why or why not?

    _____
    _____
    _____

3. What does this map tell you about the culture, mobility, settlement, and history of the United States? Why is the "Southern" dialect so distinctive here?

    _____
    _____
    _____

FIGURE 4.17. The environment provides linguistic refuge in the Caucasus Mountains

1. The world has witnessed a secessionist movement in the region of Chechnya in the past decade. In which independent country is Chechnya located and what is the language family subgroup of the Chechen language?

    _____
    _____
    _____

2. Can you determine an east-west spatial pattern among two of the language family subgroups? What is it?

    _____
    _____
    _____

3. Does this map show greater diversity of languages in terrains at higher elevations or in those at lower elevations? (You will probably need an atlas to find the answer.) Can you explain the basis for the spatial patterns?

    _____
    _____
    _____

4. Find the areas where Georgian and Ossetian are spoken. What does this tell you about the Russia-Georgia conflict in 2008? How was language a factor?

_____

_____

_____

FIGURE 4.23. Generic place-names reveal the migration of Yankee New Englanders

1. Study the map. Can you think of any reasons, historical or physical, why the areas of upstate New York and northern Maine are practically devoid of the place-name types indicated on this map?

_____

_____

_____

2. A concentration of place-name characteristics typical of New England can be found in northeastern Ohio. Can you think of any reasons for this concentration and why other areas of Ohio have far fewer of these toponyms?

_____

_____

_____

FIGURE 4.26. Arabic toponyms in Iberia

1. Using this map, speculate about the direction of the Moorish invasion and retreat, the duration of Moorish Islamic rule in different parts of Iberia, and the main centers of former Moorish power.

_____

_____

_____

2. Based on the text reading and by using an atlas, list some present-day place-names that you consider to be of Arabic origin.

_____

_____

_____

3. Look at the place-names on a map of you home state or province. Are any toponyms derived from languages other than English? (Perhaps from Spanish, French, or Native American languages?) What do these place-names reveal to you about the history of these regions?

_____

_____

_____

CREATE YOUR PERSONAL GLOSSARY OF KEY TERMS, PEOPLE, AND PLACES

In the space below, write a definition and provide an example of each key term that is sufficient for **your understanding**. It is an excellent study habit to organize your response in three parts:

1. A formal definition or identification from the textbook

2. A definition of the key term in **your own words**

3. An example to increase your understanding of the key term

KEY TERMS, PEOPLE, AND PLACES

1. geography of languages

2. language

3. dialect

4. pidgin language

5. lingua franca

6. isoglosses

7. language culture regions

8. language hotspots

_____
_____
_____

9. language families

_____
_____
_____

10. language subfamilies

_____
_____
_____

11. Indo-European family

_____
_____
_____

12. Afro-Asiatic family

_____
_____
_____

13. polyglot

_____
_____
_____

14. Niger-Congo family

_____
_____
_____

15. Altaic family

_____
_____
_____

16. Austronesian family

_____
_____
_____

17. Sino-Tibetan family

_____

_____

_____

18. Austro-Asiatic family

_____

_____

_____

19. minor language families

_____

_____

_____

20. texting

_____

_____

_____

21. slang

_____

_____

_____

22. linguistic diffusion

_____

_____

_____

23. Indo-European diffusion

_____

_____

_____

24. Austronesian diffusion

_____

_____

_____

25. Polynesian people

_____

_____

_____

26. primordial tongues

_____
_____
_____

27. Nostratic

_____
_____
_____

28. linguistic refuge areas

_____
_____
_____

29. linguistic dominance

_____
_____
_____

30. Treaty of Tordesillas

_____
_____
_____

31. Patricia Price

_____
_____
_____

32. bilingualism

_____
_____
_____

33. Ossetia and Georgia

_____
_____
_____

34. linguistic landscapes

_____
_____
_____

35. toponyms

_____
_____
_____

36. generic and specific place-names

_____
_____
_____

37. the prefix "guada"

_____
_____

38. North American dialects

_____
_____
_____

39. Caucasus Mountains

_____
_____
_____

40. Arabic toponyms in Iberia

_____
_____
_____

41. Spanglish

_____
_____
_____

REVIEW: Self-Evaluation Tests

PART ONE: Multiple-choice

Circle the best answer for each question. When you are finished, read each question again with your selected answer. After you are satisfied with your practice test, use the Answer Key in the back of the Study Guide to check your responses.

1. Languages can be defined as:
   a. speech patterns of various ethnic groups
   b. tongues that can be mutually understood
   c. speech patterns of singular ethnic groups
   d. tongues that cannot be mutually understood
   e. a collection of recognizable and similar dialects

2. Approximately _____ languages are spoken in the world today.
   a. 850
   b. 1200
   c. 3000
   d. 4500
   e. 6000

3. One existing language may be elevated to the status of _____, or language of communication and commerce, over a wide area where it is not the mother tongue.
   a. pidgin language
   b. pidgin dialect
   c. lingua franca
   d. official or national language
   e. none of the above

4. The borders of individual word usage or pronunciations are called:
   a. linguistic culture regions
   b. isoglosses
   c. language dependency zones
   d. language continuums
   e. linguistic islands

5. Languages in the Indo-European language family do NOT include:
   a. Turkish
   b. German
   c. Farsi (Persian)
   d. English
   e. Romanian

6. Three major languages of the Semitic people are Hebrew, Amharic, and:
   a. Farsi (Persian)
   b. Syrian
   c. Turkish

d. Arabic

e. Greek

7. Swahili, an important language of East Africa, is a member of which language family?
   a. Altaic
   b. Austronesia
   c. Nilo-Saharan
   d. Niger-Congo
   e. Khoisan

8. The earliest speakers of Indo-European languages apparently lived in what is now:
   a. India
   b. Turkey
   c. Russia
   d. Germany
   e. the Fertile Crescent

9. The diffusion of which language family is strongly associated with island culture and vast expanses of ocean?
   a. Austronesian
   b. Indo-European
   c. Semitic
   d. Niger-Congo
   e. none of the above

10. The Spanish language, derived from Castile, as well as the Celtic tongues, are especially rich in words describing rough terrain, such as mountains.
    a. true
    b. false

11. A good example of a linguistic refuge area is:
    a. Poland
    b. Japan
    c. southern India
    d. South Africa
    e. the Caucasus region

12. Although physical barriers such as mountain ridges can slow groups from migrating from one place to another, they infrequently serve as linguistic borders.
    a. true
    b. false

13. The Treaty of Tordesillas divided _____ between Portuguese and Spanish control.
    a. Mexico
    b. the Caribbean realm
    c. South America
    d. Brazil
    e. Argentina

14. The top five most prevalent languages in the world does NOT include:
    a. Japanese
    b. English
    c. Arabic
    d. Chinese
    e. French

15. In Muslim lands, such as parts of India, Bangladesh, and Indonesia, the language of religious ceremony is:
    a. the local language
    b. the regional lingua franca
    c. Dravidian, Bengali, and Malay
    d. Arabic
    e. Sanskrit

16. Another term for place-names is:
    a. call signs
    b. landscape symbols
    c. toponyms
    d. signage
    e. none of the above

17. Many place-names consist of:
    a. generic parts
    b. symbolic parts
    c. specific parts
    d. both a and c
    e. none of the above

18. The place-name term "center" is frequently used in what American region?
    a. New England
    b. the Deep South
    c. the Upper Midwest
    d. California
    e. the Southwest

19. Most of the world's nearly extinct languages are found in:
    a. the Pacific realm
    b. Asia
    c. Africa
    d. the Americas
    e. Europe

20. The remnants of descriptive Arabic place-names are commonly found in regions of:
    a. Italy
    b. Greece

c. France
d. Spain
e. Hungary

21. It is a fact that language is the basis for the expression of all elements of culture.
    a. true
    b. false

22. The native people of New Zealand are the:
    a. Maori
    b. Aborigines
    c. Austronesians
    d. Micronesians
    e. Moors

PART TWO: Short-answer (probable essay-type questions)

23. Briefly list some of the major themes encompassed in the study of the geography of language.

    _____

    _____

    _____

24. What defines a language family and what are some examples?

    _____

    _____

    _____

25. List some of the language subfamilies of the Indo-European language family.

    _____

    _____

    _____

26. Briefly trace the origin and diffusion of the Indo-European language family.

    _____

    _____

    _____

27. What are some of the barriers to language diffusion?

    _____

    _____

    _____

28. What are the major regional dialects of the United States? Do you agree with these designations? Why or why not?

_____

_____

_____

29. Explain the diffusion of the languages of the Polynesian peoples, such as the Hawaiians, and why this diffusion merits special attention.

_____

_____

_____

30. What are the principle language families of Africa and the Middle East?

_____

_____

_____

31. Describe some of the relationships between the environment and vocabulary.

_____

_____

_____

32. How does language guide migration? Is this phenomenon true today? Why or why not?

_____

_____

_____

33. Provide some examples of both specific and generic toponyms.

_____

_____

_____

34. What are some place-names in the United States that are derived from Native American, French, and Spanish languages? Can you think of other toponym origins in your local region?

_____

_____

_____

35. Briefly describe the various interactions between language and habitat.

_____

_____

_____

CHAPTER FIVE

GEOGRAPHIES OF RACE AND ETHNICITY: MOSAIC OR MELTING POT?

Extended Chapter Outline (Including Key Terms)

I. Ethnic Regions
    A. Ethnic homelands and islands
    B. Ethnic neighborhoods and racialized ghettos
    C. Recent shifts in ethnic mosaics

II. Mobility and Ethnicity
    A. Migration and ethnicity
    B. Simplification and isolation

III. Globalization
    A. Long view of race and ethnicity
    B. Race and European colonization
    C. Indigenous identities in the face of globalization

IV. Nature-Culture
    A. Cultural preadaptation
    B. Habitat and the preservation of difference
    C. Environmental racism

V. Ethnic Cultural Landscape
    A. Urban ethnic landscapes
    B. Re-creation of ethnic cultural landscapes
    C. Ethnic culinary landscapes

VI. Conclusion and Doing Geography

LEARNING OBJECTIVES

After reading this chapter *and* studying the maps and illustrations, you should be able to:

1. Present examples and explain how various groups define "ethnicity."

2. Understand the definitions of, and relationships between, national character, national origin, nationality, race, and ethnicity.

3. Discuss the process and characteristics of ethnic migration and mobility.

4. Discuss ethnic settlement patterns, cultural preadaptation, and ethnic survival.

5. Describe the cultural integration of ethnicity and livelihood, employment, and foodways.

6. Identify and describe elements of the ethnic landscape, including settlement patterns and urban landscapes.

7. Distinguish between an ethnic homeland and an ethnic island.

8. Understand the processes involving ethnicity and assimilation, acculturation, and reawareness.

9. Begin to understand the role of ethnicity in your family, ancestors, and local neighborhood or region.

SELECTED MAP READING AND INTERPRETATION

This section of the Study Guide is intended to increase your map-reading and interpretation skills. It will also help you apply the text readings to visual and spatial displays of concepts, themes, and examples in human and cultural geography.

A world atlas (in print or online) will be very useful in completing this section of the Study Guide and will enhance your comprehension of the maps in the textbook. Ask your instructor to recommend an appropriate web site or atlas to purchase (or visit the map collection at your library). A world atlas is essential for your personal reference library, not only during this course, but throughout your college career.

After reading the text and studying the related map and its captions, answer the following questions.

FIGURE 5.2. Foreign-born population in the United States

1. Looking at the map, what regional patterns can you detect? Explain.

2. Why do you think that some states of New England and the Deep South have the lowest foreign-born populations?

FIGURE 5.5. Ethnic minorities in China

1. Which of the ethnic regions are homelands and which are islands? How do you know?

2. Compare this to a map of population distribution in China. Why are China's ethnic groups concentrated in sparsely populated peripheries of the country?

3. Can you predict a breakup of the People's Republic of China, similar to the collapse and partition of the Soviet Union? Based on ethnicity, what new countries would you foresee?

_____

_____

_____

4. Does this map show an example of environmental racism? Why or why not?

_____

_____

_____

FIGURE 5.6. *Acadiana, the Louisiana French homeland*

1. Compare and contrast the two maps. How are they different? Explain the methods used to collect the data and create these maps.

_____

_____

_____

2. Using other maps that show the topography and biomes of Louisiana, can you find a relationship between Acadiana and the physical environment of the state? How is the environment different in the northern half of Louisiana?

_____

_____

_____

3. Explain and differentiate these terms: Acadiana, Cajun, Creole, and Cajun French.

_____

_____

_____

FIGURE 5.7. *Selected ethnic homelands in North America*

1. What are the viable ethnic homelands and why do you think they are considered viable?

_____

_____

_____

2. What are some of the ethnic islands in the regions of ethnic island concentrations?

_____

_____

_____

3. Because they are left blank, are states such as Kentucky without ethnicity? Why or why not?

_____

_____

_____

4. Why are there no ethnic homelands indicated for Native Americans?

_____

_____

_____

FIGURE 5.8. Ethnic and national-origin groups in North America

1. What are the specific ethnic groups shown in Wisconsin?

_____

_____

_____

2. Where are the areas of Dutch ethnicity on the map?

_____

_____

_____

3. Which state shows only "English" ethnicity?

_____

_____

_____

4. Is there a relationship between the African-American ethnic area and the terrain or physical environment?

_____

_____

_____

5. Why are some large ethnic groups in America, such as Poles and Czechs, not displayed on this map?

_____

_____

_____

FIGURES 5.11, 5.12, 5.13, and 5.14. Maps of ethnicity in the United States

1. Compare these four maps. What patterns emerge? Do specific states share similar statistics?

   _____

   _____

   _____

2. Compare locations of Latino and Asian populations. What "state" patterns emerge? Why?

   _____

   _____

   _____

3. Name some reasons for the spatial patterns by state on these maps.

   _____

   _____

   _____

4. How do you think urbanization patterns in the United States affect ethnic patterns on these maps? Why? Explain.

   _____

   _____

   _____

FIGURE 5.17. Iraqis displaced by conflict

1. Can you explain or think of any reasons why Iraqi refugees do not go to bordering Iran, Saudi Arabia, or Turkey in significant numbers?

   _____

   _____

   _____

2. What are the current populations of Jordan, Lebanon, and Syria? Do the people share similar culture with Iraq? Or not?

   _____

   _____

   _____

3. What does "internally displaced" indicate on the map?

   _____

   _____

   _____

FIGURE 5.23. Ethnic pluralities in the Caucasus

1. What is the relationship between ethnicity and physical terrain in this region?

   _____

   _____

   _____

2. Why do you think there are more ethnic groups in Russia than in Armenia, Georgia, and Azerbaijan?

   _____

   _____

   _____

3. Using additional sources, what can you determine about religion, language, and ethnicity in the Caucasus region? How does this impact politics and governments?

   _____

   _____

   _____

CREATE YOUR PERSONAL GLOSSARY OF KEY TERMS, PEOPLE, AND PLACES

In the space below, write a definition and provide an example of each key term that is sufficient for **your understanding**. It is an excellent study habit to organize your response in three parts:

1. A formal definition or identification from the textbook

2. A definition of the key term in **your own words**

3. An example to increase your understanding of the key term

KEY TERMS, PEOPLE, AND PLACES

1. "The Czech Capital of Nebraska"

2. ethnicity

3. race

4. acculturation

5. assimilation

6. ethnic geography

7. racism

_____

_____

_____

8. ethnic substrate

_____

_____

_____

9. ethnic homelands

_____

_____

_____

10. ethnic islands

_____

_____

_____

11. Acadiana and Cajun

_____

_____

_____

12. Hispanic, Latino, and Spanish-American

_____

_____

_____

13. Deseret

_____

_____

_____

14. Black Belt

_____

_____

_____

15. Pennsylvania Dutch

_____

_____

_____

16. ethnic neighborhood

17. ghetto

18. Daniel Arreola's practicing geography

19. chain migration

20. ethnoburbs

21. involuntary migration

22. ethnic cleansing

23. return migration

24. cultural simplification

25. cultural preadaptation

_____

_____

_____

26. Long view of race

_____

_____

_____

27. colonization

_____

_____

_____

28. indigenous

_____

_____

_____

29. Daniel Arreola

_____

_____

_____

30. superquadra

_____

_____

_____

31. foodways

_____

_____

_____

32. cultural maladaptation

_____

_____

_____

33. tortillerías

_____

_____

_____

34. ethnic landscape

_____
_____
_____

35. ethnic cuisine

_____
_____
_____

36. Little Havana

_____
_____
_____

REVIEW: Self-Evaluation Tests

PART ONE: Multiple-choice

Circle the best answer for each question. When you are finished, read each question again with your selected answer. After you are satisfied with your practice test, use the Answer Key in the back of the Study Guide to check your responses.

1. The larger society in which an ethnic group resides is referred to as a(n):
   a. ethnic island
   b. ethnic majority
   c. host culture
   d. national majority
   e. none of the above

2. When an ethnic group adopts enough of the ways of the larger society to function, this is termed:
   a. assimilation
   b. acculturation
   c. cultural adaption
   d. preadaptation
   e. melting pot

3. A complete blending with the larger society by an ethnic group is called:
   a. assimilation
   b. acculturation
   c. cultural adaption
   d. preadaptation
   e. melting pot

4. The main difference between ethnic islands and ethnic homelands is:
   a. location
   b. spatial distribution
   c. level of cultural integration
   d. settlement patterns
   e. size

5. "Deseret" is a term used by some for the homeland of:
   a. the Louisiana French
   b. French Canadians
   c. Mexican-Americans
   d. Jewish-Americans
   e. the Mormons

6. Ethnic islands are much more numerous than homelands but are as common as ethnic substrates.
   a. true
   b. false

7. A ghetto is traditionally defined as a certain urban quarter where:
   a. people are a racial minority
   b. people are forced to live
   c. people of a minority religion live
   d. Jews traditionally live
   e. none of the above

8. The most numerous ethnic minorities in North American cities today are originally from:
   a. Africa
   b. India
   c. Mexico
   d. East Asia
   e. former Communist lands

9. When compared to the United States, which of the following ethnic or national origin groups is poorly represented in Canada?
   a. African
   b. Hispanic
   c. German
   d. Mexican
   e. all of the above

10. According to the text and tables, the largest national origin/ethnic group in the United States is:
    a. Irish
    b. English
    c. German
    d. African
    e. Italian

11. In the country of Russia, only about 80 percent of the people are ethnically Russian.
    a. true
    b. false

12. About one-third of all Canadians claim single ancestry from this ancestry group:
    a. English
    b. French
    c. German
    d. Ukrainian
    e. Scottish

13. The decision for members of an ethnic group to migrate and the actual migration usually involve:
    a. hierarchical diffusion
    b. contagious diffusion
    c. relocation diffusion
    d. chain migration
    e. all of the above

14. When ethnic immigrants introduce their culture in a new land, a profound _____ occurs.
    a. prejudice
    b. cultural simplification
    c. channelization
    d. return migration
    e. all of the above

15. The example of Finnish settlement patterns in Wisconsin represents a case of:
    a. preadaptation
    b. assimilation
    c. adaptive strategy
    d. first effective settlement
    e. none of the above

16. President Barack Obama, Selena, and Tiger Woods are all examples of people of:
    a. color
    b. Latino and Hispanic heritage
    c. multiple races
    d. dual nationality
    e. ethnic assimilation

17. The ecology of ethnic survival is often related to isolation and:
    a. language
    b. religion
    c. elevation
    d. food
    e. race

18. Light blue is a Greek ethnic color, but in Chinese urban neighborhoods the venerated and auspicious color is:
    a. black
    b. purple
    c. green
    d. red
    e. yellow

19. Green, a traditional color of ethnic Irish Catholics, is also found throughout the world in _____ neighborhoods.
    a. Japanese
    b. Russian
    c. Muslim
    d. Indian
    e. French

20. Terminology in ethnic studies is often confusing. For example, if a native white South African migrates to the United States, does he become an "African-American"? In this and many respects, definitions of ethnic identity are often ones of perception and self-recognition.
    a. true
    b. false

21. A striking, highly visible imprint on the land signifying and illustrating ethnicity is known as a(n):
    a. ethnic flag
    b. ethnic substrate
    c. mission of identity
    d. cultural heritage landmark
    e. re-creation of ethnic identity

22. The American city with the highest percentage of a foreign-born population is:
    a. New York
    b. Los Angeles
    c. Seattle
    d. Atlanta
    e. Miami

23. The genocide in Rwanda in the 1990s involved the Hutu people and the _____ people.
    a. Ugandan
    b. Mizrachim
    c. Tutsi
    d. Kikuyu
    e. Congolese

PART TWO: Short-answer (probable essay-type questions)

24. What are some of the cultural and ethnic features that make Wilbur, Nebraska, the "Czech Capital of Nebraska"?

_____

_____

_____

25. Define the terms "ethnic group" and "host culture."

_____

_____

_____

26. Explain the difference between acculturation and assimilation.

_____

_____

_____

27. What is the focus of ethnic geography studies?

_____

_____

_____

28. What are the two distinct geographical types of ethnic regions? Provide an example of each.

_____

_____

_____

29. Provide an example of an ethnic homeland and an ethnic island in North America.

_____

_____

_____

30. Explain the difference between an ethnic neighborhood and an ethnic ghetto.

_____

_____

_____

31. Why are cities in North America more ethnically diverse than any other urban centers in the world?

_____

_____

_____

32. What are the top five ethnic ancestry/national origin groups in the United States? How do these differ from those in Canada?

_____

_____

_____

33. Explain the concept of chain migration.

_____

_____

_____

34. Briefly discuss the concept of preadaptation in ethnic migration.

_____

_____

_____

35. Provide some examples of ethnic environmental racism.

_____

_____

_____

36. What is the relationship between ethnicity and business activity?

_____

_____

_____

37. What is the relationship between ethnicity and type of employment?

_____

_____

_____

38. Who and where are the Hmong-Americans, and what are their distinctive gardening practices?

_____

_____

_____

39. What is an example of an "ethnic flag"?

_____

_____

_____

40. How can colors connote and reveal ethnicity? Provide examples.

_____

_____

_____

41. What are some of the contributions of Professor Daniel Arreola?

_____

_____

_____

42. What are some local examples of ethnicity in your home town, city, or region?

_____

_____

_____

43. Nearly everyone in North America is part of some ethnic fabric or identity. Describe the role of ethnicity or ethnic ancestry in your family or acquaintances.

_____

_____

_____

CHAPTER SIX

POLITICAL GEOGRAPHY: A DIVIDED WORLD

Extended Chapter Outline (Including Key Terms)

I.   Political Geography Regions
    A. Independent states
       1. Territoriality
       2. Boundaries
       3. Spatial organization
       4. Cyberspace
    B. Supranational political bodies
    C. Electoral geography

II. Mobility and Political Geography
    A. Core and periphery
    B. Mobility, diffusion, and innovations
    C. Migration

III. Globalization
    A. The nation-state
    B. Ethnic separatism
    C. The cleavage model
    D. Example: Sakha Republic
    E. Political imprint on economic geography

IV. Nature-Culture
    A. Geopolitics
    B. Heartland theory
    C. Geopolitics today
    D. Warfare and the environment

V. Political Cultural Landscapes
    A. Imprint of the legal code
    B. Physical properties of boundaries
    C. The impress of central authority
    D. National iconography on the landscape

VI. Conclusion and Doing Geography

LEARNING OBJECTIVES

After reading this chapter *and* studying the maps and illustrations, you should be able to:

1. Describe various types of states, countries, and other political bodies.

2. Understand the themes and concepts associated with country building and borders.

3. Explain the political ecology of warfare and environmental destruction, the Cleavage model, and Mackinder's heartland theory.

4. Explain the relationship of ethnicity and territory to the nation-state and the multinational and supranational state.

5. Describe the effects of political decision making on the cultural landscape.

6. Provide examples of the basic elements of the political landscape such as the boundary.

7. Better understand many of the world's current geopolitics, political conflicts, and wars, based on your knowledge of political and cultural geography.

SELECTED MAP READING AND INTERPRETATION

This section of the Study Guide is intended to increase your map-reading and interpretation skills. It will also help you apply the text readings to visual and spatial displays of concepts, themes, and examples in human and cultural geography.

A world atlas (in print or online) will be very useful in completing this section of the Study Guide and will enhance your comprehension of the maps in the textbook. Ask your instructor to recommend an appropriate web site or atlas to purchase (or visit the map collection at your library). A world atlas is essential for your personal reference library, not only during this course, but throughout your college career.

After reading the text and studying the related map and its captions, answer the following questions.

FIGURE 6.1. The independent countries of the world

1. The United States basically shares a border with only two countries. How many countries now border Russia and what are they? (Don't forget Norway!)

_____

_____

_____

2. What are the independent countries of Central Asia and the Caucasus region that were part of the Soviet Union until the early 1990s?

_____

_____

_____

3. Which independent countries were derived from the breakup of Yugoslavia, of Ethiopia, and of Czechoslovakia in the 1990s?

_____

_____

_____

4. Locate these independent countries on the world map: Bhutan, Sierra Leone, Oman, French Guiana, Slovenia, Lithuania, Belize, Papua New Guinea, Swaziland, Haiti, and Vanuatu.

_____

_____

_____

_____

FIGURE 6.3. Two independent countries, A and B

1. These are real countries. Using an atlas, identify them. This may be challenging to some!

   _____
   _____
   _____

2. The conditions shown and described here are for 1994. What was the territorial outcome of this dispute? Today?

   _____
   _____
   _____

3. What and where are the actual religions, languages, and ethnicities of the various territories shown on this map?

   _____
   _____
   _____

FIGURE 6.5. Some supranational political organizations in the Eastern Hemisphere

1. Can you identify the reasons why certain European countries, such as Norway, Switzerland, Albania, and Turkey, are *not* part of the European Union?

   _____
   _____
   _____

2. Are all the member countries of the Arab League located in the Middle East? What is the status of the country between Morocco and Mauritania?

   _____
   _____
   _____

3. What territories of the former Soviet Union are *not* part of the Commonwealth of Independent States? Why are they not?

   _____
   _____
   _____

FIGURE 6.6. The electoral geography of Europe

1. What are the major clusters (in red) of strongly leftist/socialist voting in western Europe? Can you explain any reasons for this, based on economics or geography?

    _____

    _____

    _____

2. The strongly rightist/conservative voting areas in much of continental Europe are located in the Alps (Swiss, French, Austrian, German, Italian), the Pyrenees, and the Jura and Tatra mountains. Can you think of any reasons based on culture and land why this pattern exists?

    _____

    _____

    _____

FIGURE 6.13. Russia developed from a core area

1. Can you think of reasons why expansion to the east was greater than to the west? What were the barriers?

    _____

    _____

    _____

2. What environmental goals might have motivated Russian expansion?

    _____

    _____

    _____

3. What were the causes behind the recent contraction of the country? Do you foresee any further contraction?

    _____

    _____

    _____

FIGURE 6.14. Independence from European colonial rule

1. Can you identify some barriers that slowed the diffusion of independence in Africa?

    _____

    _____

    _____

2. 1960 was a landmark year for African independence. Using other maps, can you identify areas of British, French, Belgian, and Portuguese rule in Africa and show whether a relationship exists between colonial ruler and year of independence?

_____
_____
_____

3. Why did independence come so late to Namibia? Can you find any reasons for this? Who were the colonial rulers of Namibia?

_____
_____
_____

4. List all the countries that became independent before 1960 and their respective year of sovereignty. (Also identify the Arab countries included here.)

_____
_____
_____

FIGURE 6.16. *Nation-states, multinational countries, and other types*

1. Identify 10 nation-states from this map.

_____
_____
_____

2. Why are the countries of Great Britain and Spain classified as old multinational states?

_____
_____
_____

3. What is your opinion about the United States as a country evolving toward nation-statehood?

_____
_____
_____

4. This classification of nation-statehood is arbitrary and debatable. How would you change it, and why?

_____
_____
_____

FIGURE 6.19. Kurdistan

1. In what countries are areas of Kurdish predominance found?

_____

_____

_____

2. Using your atlas, can you identify the physical landscape of Kurdistan and thus show that a folk fortress situation exists?

_____

_____

_____

3. Why and how does this map show reasons for political instability in this region? Is this especially true for Iraq and Iran? Why or why not?

_____

_____

_____

4. If Kurdistan become an independent country, what problems of a geopolitical nature, such as access to the seas, may they have?

_____

_____

_____

CREATE YOUR PERSONAL GLOSSARY OF KEY TERMS, PEOPLE, AND PLACES

In the space below, write a definition and provide an example of each key term that is sufficient for **your understanding**. It is an excellent study habit to organize your response in three parts:

1. A formal definition or identification from the textbook

2. A definition of the key term in **your own words**

3. An example to increase your understanding of the key term

KEY TERMS, PEOPLE, AND PLACES

1. political geography

_____
_____
_____

2. independent countries

_____
_____
_____

3. political culture region

_____
_____
_____

4. territoriality

_____
_____
_____

5. nationalism

_____
_____
_____

6. national territory

_____
_____
_____

7. enclave and exclave

_____

_____

_____

8. Afrikaans

_____

_____

_____

9. boundaries

_____

_____

_____

10. marchlands

_____

_____

_____

11. buffer state

_____

_____

_____

12. satellite state

_____

_____

_____

13. natural boundaries

_____

_____

_____

14. ethnographic boundaries

_____

_____

_____

15. geometric boundaries

_____

_____

_____

16. unitary and federal spatial organization

17. centripetal forces

18. centrifugal forces

19. raison d'être

20. supranational organizations

21. electoral geography

22. cleavages

23. cyberspace

24. political mobility

25. secession movements

_____
_____
_____

26. diffusion of insurgencies and innovations

_____
_____
_____

27. political ecology

_____
_____
_____

28. folk fortress

_____
_____
_____

29. manifest destiny

_____
_____
_____

30. heartland theory

_____
_____
_____

31. Halford Mackinder

_____
_____
_____

32. rimland

_____
_____
_____

33. red and blue states

_____
_____
_____

34. nation-state

_____

_____

_____

35. multinational country

_____

_____

_____

36. ethnic separatism

_____

_____

_____

37. cleavage model

_____

_____

_____

38. Kurdistan

_____

_____

_____

39. political imprint

_____

_____

_____

40. Islamic law

_____

_____

_____

41. imprint of the legal code

_____

_____

_____

42. border landscapes

_____

_____

_____

43. impress of central authority

_____
_____
_____

44. national iconography

_____
_____
_____

45. Great Wall of China

_____
_____
_____

46. Mount Rushmore

_____
_____
_____

REVIEW: Self-Evaluation Tests

PART ONE: Multiple-choice

Circle the best answer for each question. When you are finished, read each question again with your selected answer. After you are satisfied with your practice test, use the Answer Key in the back of the Study Guide to check your responses.

1. Earth's surface is divided into approximately _____ independent countries.
   a. 230
   b. 320
   c. 280
   d. 200
   e. 190

2. Europe and Africa each have about the same number of independent countries.
   a. true
   b. false

3. Theoretically, the most desirable shape for a country is:
   a. elongated
   b. square
   c. hexagonal
   d. triangular
   e. none of the above

4. Which of the following are areas of national territory separated from the main body of a country by the territory of another?
   a. peninsulas
   b. exclaves
   c. enclaves
   d. colonies
   e. protectorates

5. Until quite recently, many boundaries were not clear or sharp, but undefined, somewhat fuzzy zones called:
   a. buffer states
   b. frontiers
   c. hinterlands
   d. marchlands
   e. international zones

6. Mongolia and Nepal serve as good examples of:
   a. "shoestring" countries
   b. buffer states
   c. secessionist states
   d. satellite states

e. rump or truncated states

7. Boundaries that are based on neither cultural nor physical features are often:
   a. ethnographic
   b. geometric
   c. natural
   d. irregular
   e. none of the above

8. An excellent example of a relic boundary exists:
   a. between Canada and Alaska
   b. between Brazil and Argentina
   c. between Laos and Cambodia
   d. within Germany
   e. within Ireland

9. A federal government is usually considered a less geographically expressive system.
   a. true
   b. false

10. The United States, Canada, France, and Australia are all examples of federal governments.
    a. true
    b. false

11. Whatever disrupts internal order and encourages destruction of the country is called:
    a. a raison d'être
    b. insurgency
    c. centrifugal force
    d. nationalism
    e. centripetal force

12. Electoral geography is useful for identifying:
    a. the Lower South
    b. formal and functional culture regions
    c. spatial patterns of ethnicity
    d. supranational organizations
    e. none of the above

13. The creation of districts that have a majority of voters favoring the group in power and a minority of opposition voters is called:
    a. gerrymandering
    b. cleavage-control districts
    c. redistricting
    d. raison d'être
    e. selective electoral districts

14. During political diffusion, the original core area seldom remains the country's most important district.
    a. true
    b. false

15. The Russian state originated in the small principality of:
    a. St. Petersburg
    b. Kiev
    c. Warsaw
    d. Novgorod
    e. Moscow

16. Countries without political core areas, such as Zaire and Belgium, are potentially the least stable of all independent states.
    a. true
    b. false

17. The best example of contagious expansion diffusion in political geography is:
    a. the growth of the Russian Empire
    b. political independence in Africa
    c. the creation of Mexico
    d. British colonization of India
    e. the reunification of Germany

18. Throughout much of history, a country's survival was enhanced by some sort of natural protection. These areas of protection are called:
    a. national moats
    b. natural defenses
    c. ethnic islands
    d. national shields
    e. folk fortresses

19. The "heartland theory" was developed by geographer:
    a. Wilbur Zelinsky
    b. Hubert Wilhelm
    c. Halford Mackinder
    d. Hubertus Bloemer
    e. Derwent Whittlesey

20. The heartland theory predicted, in effect:
    a. the growth of Southern Democrats
    b. the economic power of the Midwest
    c. the rise of French and British colonialism
    d. Russian conquest of the world
    e. Communism in mainland China

21. Which of the following is NOT an example of a modern nation-state?
    a. Sweden
    b. Belgium
    c. Japan
    d. Armenia
    e. Germany

22. The greatest concentration of the Francophone cultural-linguistic minority in Canada is found in:
    a. Toronto
    b. Ontario
    c. Manitoba
    d. Newfoundland and New Brunswick
    e. Québec

23. The "impress of central authority" refers to:
    a. usually unitary rather than federal states
    b. transportation networks
    c. omnipresent military authority
    d. government and landscape
    e. none of the above

24. A good example of national iconography in the American landscape is:
    a. bald eagles and flags
    b. the National Cathedral
    c. the Grand Canyon
    d. New York City
    e. baseball

25. This former principality is used as an example to illustrate the relationship between terrain and political geography:
    a. Andorra
    b. Liechtenstein
    c. Bavaria
    d. Berchtesgaden
    e. Denmark

26. Based on the 2008 presidential election in the United States, all of the "blue states" are located on major bodies of water, except four, including:
    a. Missouri
    b. Vermont
    c. Arizona
    d. Utah
    e. Louisiana

SELECTED MAP READING AND INTERPRETATION

This section of the Study Guide is intended to increase your map-reading and interpretation skills. It will also help you apply the text readings to visual and spatial displays of concepts, themes, and examples in human and cultural geography.

A world atlas (in print or online) will be very useful in completing this section of the Study Guide and will enhance your comprehension of the maps in the textbook. Ask your instructor to recommend an appropriate web site or atlas to purchase (or visit the map collection at your library). A world atlas is essential for your personal reference library, not only during this course, but throughout your college career.

After reading the text and studying the related map and its captions, answer the following questions.

FIGURE 7.3. The world distribution of major religions

1. Other than in some African countries, where is animism evident in the world?

_____
_____
_____

2. What are the primarily Protestant countries of Europe?

_____
_____
_____

3. Is Hinduism limited to India? If not, where else is it found?

_____
_____
_____

4. Describe the changes in major religions of Africa, from north to south.

_____
_____
_____

FIGURE 7.4. Distribution of religious groups in Lebanon

1. What are the geographic patterns of religious groups in Lebanon?

_____
_____
_____

2. Can you think of reasons why Lebanon serves as a religious refuge area? What is the pattern of the physical terrain?

_____

_____

_____

3. Explain the differences among the three branches of Christianity found in Lebanon.

_____

_____

_____

FIGURE 7.7. Leading Christian denominations in the United States and Canada

1. Can you explain the patterns of religion in Texas and Louisiana?

_____

_____

_____

2. Why do you think that Lutheranism is most prevalent in the Upper Midwest?

_____

_____

_____

3. Can you explain why some states, such as Ohio, have no denominational majority, while others, such as Utah and Mississippi, have basically one majority?

_____

_____

_____

4. Other than Catholic, Baptist, and Lutheran majority areas, what other regional patterns are evident?

_____

_____

_____

5. Where is a Mennonite majority located? Does this include the Amish people, too?

_____

_____

_____

FIGURE 7.15. The diffusion of Christianity in Europe, first to eleventh centuries

1. Look at the patterns of diffusion by the year 300. In what way do these patterns suggest hierarchical expansion diffusion?

_____

_____

_____

2. What barriers to diffusion might account for the uneven advance of Christianity by the year 1050?

_____

_____

_____

3. What were the last "pagan" countries of Europe? They were not Christianized until the late fourteenth century.

_____

_____

_____

FIGURE 7.23. Secularized areas in Europe

1. Look at German-speaking countries (Austria, Germany, Switzerland, Liechtenstein). What patterns prevail in secularization? Can you identify an east-west and/or a north-south pattern?

_____

_____

_____

2. Can you account for any reasons or similarities among regions where religion is most widely practiced?

_____

_____

_____

FIGURE 7.27. Consumption and avoidance of pork are influenced by religion

1. Can you explain the pattern in the United States? Think of factors of economy and culture.

_____

_____

_____

2. How do these global patterns correspond to the map (Figure 7.3) of major world religions?

_____

_____

_____

CREATE YOUR PERSONAL GLOSSARY OF KEY TERMS, PEOPLE, AND PLACES

In the space below, write a definition and provide an example of each key term that is sufficient for **your understanding**. It is an excellent study habit to organize your response in three parts:

1. A formal definition or identification from the textbook

2. a definition of the key term in **your own words**

3. An example to increase your understanding of the key term

KEY TERMS, PEOPLE, AND PLACES

1. religion

2. proselytic religions

3. ethnic religions

4. sacred space

5. spiritual places

6. fundamentalism

7. monotheism and polytheism

_____
_____
_____

8. Western Christianity

_____
_____
_____

9. Eastern Christianity

_____
_____
_____

10. Coptic church

_____
_____
_____

11. Maronites

_____
_____
_____

12. syncretic religions

_____
_____
_____

13. Eastern Orthodoxy

_____
_____
_____

14. Protestantism

_____
_____
_____

15. Bible Belt

_____
_____
_____

16. Islam

_____

_____

_____

17. The Qur'an

_____

_____

_____

18. The Five Pillars of Islam

_____

_____

_____

19. Shi'ite and Sunni Muslims

_____

_____

_____

20. Judaism

_____

_____

_____

21. Sephardim and Ashkenazim

_____

_____

_____

22. Hinduism

_____

_____

_____

23. Jainism

_____

_____

_____

24. Sikhism

_____

_____

_____

25. Buddhism

_____
_____
_____

26. Confucianism

_____
_____
_____

27. Taoist religions

_____
_____
_____

28. Shintoism and Lamaism

_____
_____
_____

29. Animism and shamanism

_____
_____
_____

30. secularization

_____
_____
_____

31. Semitic religious hearth

_____
_____
_____

32. East Asian religious hearth

_____
_____
_____

33. contact conversion

_____
_____
_____

34. Indus-Ganges religious hearth

_____

_____

_____

35. religious ecology

_____

_____

_____

36. Gaia hypothesis

_____

_____

_____

37. Kenneth Foote

_____

_____

_____

38. "shadowed ground"

_____

_____

_____

39. doctrine of ahimsa

_____

_____

_____

40. food taboos

_____

_____

_____

41. Evangelical Protestantism

_____

_____

_____

42. pilgrimage

_____

_____

_____

43. Lourdes, France

_____
_____
_____

44. Mecca, Saudi Arabia

_____
_____
_____

45. Ganges River

_____
_____
_____

46. theocracy

_____
_____
_____

47. sacred landscapes

_____
_____
_____

48. mosques and minarets

_____
_____
_____

49. Mennonites and Mormons

_____
_____
_____

REVIEW: Self-Evaluation Tests

PART ONE: Multiple-choice

Circle the best answer for each question. When you are finished, read each question again with your selected answer. After you are satisfied with your practice test, use the Answer Key in the back of the Study Guide to check your responses.

1. Religion can be defined as:
    a. cultural theory
    b. a set of beliefs
    c. worship of either one or many gods
    d. a way of life
    e. a form of organized cult

2. Religions that seek new members are termed:
    a. aggressive
    b. growth active
    c. proselytic
    d. charismatic
    e. ethnic religions

3. Judaism and Hinduism may be termed:
    a. aggressive
    b. growth active
    c. proselytic
    d. charismatic
    e. ethnic religions

4. An example of sacred space is:
    a. Dome of the Rock
    b. a Christian church
    c. the Wailing Wall
    d. all of the above
    e. none of the above

5. Islam may be termed a(n) _____ faith.
    a. polytheistic
    b. vernacular
    c. monotheistic
    d. ethnic
    e. none of the above

6. Christian Egyptians are often members of the Eastern group of Christianity called:
    a. the Coptic church
    b. Maronites
    c. Eastern Orthodox
    d. Melkites

e. Nestorians

7. Most of the Christians of the highland region of Lebanon are:
   a. Copts
   b. Nestorians
   c. Greek Orthodox
   d. Maronites
   e. Presbyterians

8. The core of the Latter-Day Saints realm is:
   a. Nevada
   b. Missouri
   c. South Dakota
   d. North Dakota
   e. Utah

9. Who among the following is considered a prophet of Islam?
   a. Jesus
   b. Moses
   c. Mohammad
   d. Abraham
   e. all of the above

10. The stronghold of the Shi'ite branch of Islam is the country of:
    a. Iraq
    b. Iran
    c. Saudi Arabia
    d. Kuwait
    e. Libya

11. The Jews who eventually settled in central and eastern Europe were known as the:
    a. Ashkenazim
    b. Orthodox
    c. Hasidic
    d. Sephardim
    e. none of the above

12. The majority of the world's Jewish population lives in:
    a. Europe
    b. Israel
    c. Russia
    d. North America
    e. Poland and Romania

13. The concept of "ahimsa" is focused on the:
    a. caste system
    b. Dravidian ethnic divide
    c. idea of nirvana

d. veneration of all life forms

e. Five Pillars of Islam

14. Hinduism has splintered into diverse religious groups that are usually regarded as separate religions. Two major direct splinter groups are:

    a. Lamaism and Sikhism

    b. Taoism and Lamaism

    c. Coptic and Nestorian

    d. Sikhism and Jainism

    e. none of the above

15. Buddhism is a religion derived from Taoism.

    a. true

    b. false

16. Lamaism prevails not only in Tibet, but also in:

    a. Nepal

    b. Mongolia

    c. China

    d. Thailand

    e. all of the above

17. People who are considered _____ in their form of faith believe that rocks, rivers, and other natural features can possess spirits or souls.

    a. monotheistic

    b. theocratic

    c. animistic

    d. secularized

    e. heathen

18. The youngest religion of the Semitic religious hearth is:

    a. Islam

    b. Judaism

    c. Hinduism

    d. Christianity

    e. Sikhism

19. The use of missionaries primarily involves the concept of:

    a. hierarchical diffusion

    b. relocation diffusion

    c. distance-decay

    d. eminent domain

    e. all of the above

20. What is the process of religious diffusion called in the case when political leaders (such as kings) are converted to Christianity and their subjects later follow?

    a. hierarchical diffusion

    b. relocation diffusion

c. distance-decay
d. eminent domain
e. all of the above

21. Buddhism, although strongly associated with the lands and people of southeastern and eastern Asia such as China and Laos, actually began in the Indian subcontinent.
a. true
b. false

22. Which geographer is especially interested in "shadowed ground," a place where tragedy has occurred?
a. Pradyumna Karan
b. Mike Kukral
c. Kenneth Foote
d. Ted Bernard
e. Hugh Bloemer

23. Chinese Buddhists originally invented the magnetic compass to serve the needs of reincarnation and the travel of the soul.
a. true
b. false

24. A "Love Your Mother" bumper sticker is a good example of viewing the Earth as a mother figure. This is related to:
a. reincarnation theory
b. Edgar Cayce
c. the Gaia hypothesis
d. Zoroastrianism
e. Protestant evangelicalism

25. Many followers of Islam make religious pilgrimages to the holy cities of Mecca and:
a. Jiddah
b. Riyadh
c. Damascus
d. Cairo
e. Medina

26. In India and elsewhere, the word "ghat" refers to:
a. any structure of sacred worship
b. a sacred space reserved for the burying of the dead
c. steps that often lead down to water
d. pagan or heathen regions of "nonbelievers"
e. a balance or harmony of human and nature

PART TWO: Short answer (probable essay-type questions)

27. Provide examples of proselytic and ethnic religions and discuss the difference them.

_____
_____
_____

28. What are some of the general spatial patterns of religion in North America?

_____
_____
_____

29. What are some of the characteristics of the Islamic faith?

_____
_____
_____

30. What is polytheism and what are some examples of this form of religion?

_____
_____
_____

31. Briefly discuss the origin and diffusion of Buddhism, including its fusion with native ethnic religions.

_____
_____
_____

32. What are some common characteristics of animism and where can it be found today?

_____
_____
_____

33. Briefly discuss theories regarding the origin of religions in the Semitic religious hearth.

_____
_____
_____

34. Provide examples of the mobility of religion.

_____
_____
_____

35. What religions grew out of the Indus-Ganges religious hearth?

_____
_____
_____

36. What are some barriers to the diffusion of religion?

_____

_____

_____

37. What are the practices of ecotheology and how do they relate to the physical environment?

_____

_____

_____

38. What is the religious significance of Mount Shasta in California?

_____

_____

_____

39. How are environmental factors used to explain the origin of monotheistic faiths?

_____

_____

_____

40. Explain Professor Foote's "Shadowed Ground."

_____

_____

_____

41. How can religion influence people's perception of the environment?

_____

_____

_____

42. Explain the use of fish and wine in Christianity as examples of the relationship between religion and economy.

_____

_____

_____

43. What are the various food taboos among Hindus, Muslims, Mormons, and Jews?

_____

_____

_____

44. What is the purpose of a religious pilgrimage and what are some very important pilgrimage sites for Jews, Muslims, and Christians?

_____

_____

_____

45. Discuss Patricia Price's observations regarding Jerusalem:

_____

_____

_____

_____

46. How do cemeteries preserve truly ancient cultural traits? Provide some examples.

_____

_____

_____

CHAPTER EIGHT

AGRICULTURE: THE GEOGRAPHY OF THE GLOBAL FOOD SYSTEM

Extended Chapter Outline (Including Key Terms)

I. Agricultural Regions
    A. Swidden cultivation
    B. Paddy rice farming
    C. Peasant grain, root, and livestock farming
    D. Plantation agriculture
    E. Market gardening
    F. Livestock fattening
    G. Grain farming
    H. Dairying
    I. Nomadic herding
    J. Livestock ranching
    L. Urban agriculture
    M. Farming the waters

II. Mobility of Agriculture
    A. Origins and diffusion of plant domestication
    B. Tracing animal domestication
    C. Modern mobility and the green revolution
    D. Labor mobility

III. Globalization of Agriculture
    A. Local-global food provisioning
    B. The von Thünen model
    C. Feeding the world
    D. Growth of agribusiness
    E. Food fears

IV. Nature-Culture and Agriculture
    A. Technology over nature?
    B. Sustainable agriculture
    C. Land use and desertification
    D. Environmental perception by agriculturists
    E. Organic foods and green fuels

V. Agricultural Landscapes
    A. Survey, cadastral, and field patterns
    B. Fencing
    C. Hedging

VI. Conclusion and Suggested Readings

LEARNING OBJECTIVES

After reading this chapter *and* studying the maps and illustrations, you should be able to:

1. Describe various forms of agriculture, such as subsistence agriculture and commercial livestock fattening.

2. Trace the origin and places of plant and animal domestication.

3. Discuss the contributions of several important scholars, including von Thünen, to the study of agriculture.

4. Explain and understand the mobility of agriculture from one region or continent to another.

5. Describe the influence of the environment on agricultural practices and how humans modify the earth to suit their agricultural needs and methods.

6. Understand and explain the role of human and environmental perception on land use and agricultural production.

7. Discuss the effects of globalization and genetically modified (GM) crops on feeding the world.

8. Provide examples from around the world of various agricultural lifestyles and practices.

9. Understand the various techniques of land survey, land division, fencing, and hedging that shape the cultural landscape.

10. Continue to sharpen your skills in map reading and interpretation.

SELECTED MAP READING AND INTERPRETATION

This section of the Study Guide is intended to increase your map-reading and interpretation skills. It will also help you apply the text readings to visual and spatial displays of concepts, themes, and examples in human and cultural geography.

A world atlas (in print or online) will be very useful in completing this section of the Study Guide and will enhance your comprehension of the maps in the textbook. Ask your instructor to recommend an appropriate web site or atlas to purchase (or visit the map collection at your library). A world atlas is essential for your personal reference library, not only during this course, but throughout your college career.

After reading the text and studying the related map and its captions, answer the following questions.

FIGURE 8.3. Two agricultural regions in China

1. Where would you draw the cultural boundary between the two types of agriculture? What might account for this north-south pattern?

   _____
   _____
   _____

2. Find a population density and distribution map of China (see Chapter 3) and compare it to regions of agriculture. What are your findings? Also, can you find a relationship to major rivers and agriculture type?

   _____
   _____
   _____

FIGURE 8.12. Global aquaculture and fisheries

1. In addition to China and India, what are the leading countries in aquaculture production?

   _____
   _____
   _____

2. Why do you think Australia ranks so low in aquaculture despite having a significant coastline? What other countries are low in production? Why?

   _____
   _____
   _____

FIGURE 8.13. Ancient centers of plant domestication

1. Why should this map be regarded as theoretical or speculative?

    _____

    _____

    _____

2. What is the historic name of the region acknowledged as the hearth area of the earliest plant and animal domestication in the Middle East region? Do some research.

    _____

    _____

    _____

3. Where are the regions of domestication of plants in the Americas? What vegetables were domesticated here and what was their possible path of diffusion?

    _____

    _____

    _____

FIGURE 8.18. Ideal and actual distribution of types of agriculture in Uruguay

1. In what ways does the spatial pattern of Uruguayan agriculture conform to von Thünen's model?

    _____

    _____

    _____

2. How is the pattern of agriculture in Uruguay different from von Thünen's model and what might cause the anomalies?

    _____

    _____

    _____

FIGURE 8.19. Mapping hunger worldwide

1. What geographic patterns does this map show?

    _____

    _____

    _____

2. Can you explain the pattern in Africa? Why do you think North Africa (in the same category as the United States) is different from other regions of Africa?

    _____

    _____

    _____

FIGURE 8.21. Worldwide use of genetically altered crop plants

1. Do you think there are similar reasons for the similar patterns in Europe and Africa? Explain.

    _____
    _____
    _____

2. What does this map tell you about agriculture in the Western Hemisphere? Family farms? Commercial farms? Scale of farms?

    _____
    _____
    _____

FIGURE 8.25. Risk of desertification in Africa

1. Which countries are facing the most severe desertification?

    _____
    _____
    _____

2. Using other maps, identify the general climate types, wind patterns, and topography in the three divisions of desertification on this map.

    _____
    _____
    _____

3. What are the contrasting rainfall regions in the yellow areas of this map? Why is desertification not a problem in many areas of the Sahara or in the rainforest of the Congo Basin?

    _____
    _____
    _____

FIGURE 8.29. Original land-survey patterns in the United States and Canada

1. Even if you live in a big city now, identify your local original survey system and describe it:

    _____
    _____
    _____

2. Explain why the metes and bounds system is found primarily in the original 13 colonies of America.

_____

_____

_____

CREATE YOUR PERSONAL GLOSSARY OF KEY TERMS, PEOPLE, AND PLACES

In the space below, write a definition and provide an example of each key term that is sufficient for **your understanding**. It is an excellent study habit to organize your response in three parts:

1. A formal definition or identification from the textbook

2. A definition of the key term in **your own words**

3. An example to increase your understanding of the key term

KEY TERMS, PEOPLE, AND PLACES

1. agriculture

2. agricultural regions

3. swidden cultivation

4. slash-and-burn agriculture

5. intercropping

6. subsistence agriculture

7. paddy rice farming

_____

8. double-cropping

_____

9. green revolution

_____

10. Mediterranean agriculture

_____

11. nomadic herding

_____

12. plantation agriculture

_____

13. luxury crops

_____

14. metes and bounds survey

_____

15. market gardening

_____

16. Corn Belt

_____

_____

_____

17. feedlots and commercial livestock fattening

_____

_____

_____

18. commercial grain farming

_____

_____

_____

19. biofuels

_____

_____

_____

20. dairying and livestock ranching

_____

_____

_____

21. hunting and gathering groups

_____

_____

_____

22. aquaculture

_____

_____

_____

23. environmental perception by agriculturalists

_____

_____

_____

24. GM crops

_____

_____

_____

25. agricultural productivity per capita

_____
_____
_____

26. Johann Heinrich von Thünen

_____
_____
_____

27. isolated state model

_____
_____
_____

28. mariculture

_____
_____
_____

29. desertification

_____
_____
_____

30. Thomas Malthus

_____
_____
_____

31. cadastral pattern

_____
_____
_____

32. survey patterns

_____
_____
_____

33. fragmented landholding

_____
_____
_____

34. U.S. rectangular survey system

_____
_____
_____

35. peasant

_____
_____
_____

36. migrant workers

_____
_____
_____

37. open-field areas

_____
_____
_____

38. hedgerow country

_____
_____
_____

39. domesticated plant

_____
_____
_____

40. Sahel Zone

_____
_____
_____

41. Fertile Crescent

_____
_____
_____

42. long-lot settlement

_____
_____
_____

43. domesticated animal

44. "gene banks"

45. cool chains

46. cultural preadaptation

47. modification of the environment by agriculturalists

48. the global chicken

49. agribusiness

50. food fears

REVIEW: Self-Evaluation Tests

PART ONE: Multiple-choice

Circle the best answer for each question. When you are finished, read each question again with your selected answer. After you are satisfied with your practice test, use the Answer Key in the back of the Study Guide to check your responses.

1. About _____ percent of the world's working population is employed in agriculture.
    a. 2   b. 5   c. 15   d. 30   e. 40

2. In the United States, the number of people involved in farming is less than _____ percent.
    a. 3   b. 20   c. 10   d. 12   e. 15

3. The agricultural practice of shifting cultivation is essentially:
    a. "slash-and-burn" agriculture
    b. a land-rotation system
    c. found in Russia and other former communist states
    d. subsistence agriculture
    e. none of the above

4. The hallmark of paddy rice farming is:
    a. Irish stone fences
    b. environmental deterioration
    c. high protein productivity
    d. terraced paddy fields
    e. the water buffalo

5. Planting and harvesting the same land 2 or 3 times a year is known as:
    a. intertillage
    b. crop rotation
    c. double-cropping
    d. biannual agriculture
    e. none of the above

6. The "green revolution" involved the introduction of:
    a. sugar cane
    b. chemical fertilizers
    c. organic methods
    d. traditional practices of sustainability
    e. gene banks

7. Llamas and alpacas serve as traditional beasts of burden in:
    a. South America
    b. Mexico

c. the Middle East and North Africa

d. Southeast Asia

e. Southeast Ohio

8. Traditional Mediterranean agriculture is based in part on the cultivation of primarily barley and:

a. oats

b. millet

c. rye

d. wheat

e. rice

9. Nomadic herding is normally practiced in what type of environment?

a. fertile valley floors

b. tropical rain forests

c. mountains or deserts

d. coastal plains

e. temperate forests

10. Plantation agriculture usually maximizes the production of _____ for Europeans and Americans.

a. coffee and tea

b. grains

c. cattle and other livestock

d. luxury crops

e. fruits and vegetables

11. Crops that tend to grow best in tropical highland regions are:

a. coffee and tea

b. grains

c. luxury crops

d. fruits and vegetables

e. none of the above

12. Market gardening is also referred to as:

a. neo-plantation

b. greenhouse farming

c. truck farming

d. market plantation

e. organic farming

13. One of the most highly developed areas of commercial livestock fattening is:

a. Alpine Europe

b. the Mediterranean region

c. the northeastern United States

d. the Corn Belt

e. Mesoamerica

14. Fattening livestock, especially cattle, is an efficient method of protein production.
    a. true
    b. false

15. The major wheat-producing countries (producing 35 percent of the world's wheat) are the United States, Russia, Canada, Argentina, Kazakhstan, and:
    a. Germany
    b. Australia
    c. India
    d. Italy
    e. Ukraine

16. Dairy farms located near large urban areas usually produce:
    a. butter
    b. cheese
    c. yogurt
    d. processed milk
    e. none of the above

17. Australia, New Zealand, South Africa, and Argentina produce 70 percent of the world's exports of:
    a. beef
    b. wool
    c. coffee and tea
    d. pork
    e. fruit crops

18. Mad cow disease is an example involving the issue of:
    a. GM foods
    b. food fears
    c. agribusiness
    d. feedlot disease
    e. salmonella

19. Perhaps the oldest primary region of agriculture is:
    a. Southeast Asia
    b. northwestern India
    c. the Fertile Crescent
    d. Mesoamerica
    e. northeastern China

20. The diffusion of many plant crops from the Western Hemisphere was accomplished by colonial powers, such as the Dutch and the Portuguese.
   a. true
   b. false

21. What was developed to preserve the remaining domesticated plant varieties?
   a. hybrid seeds
   b. the green revolution
   c. gene banks
   d. agriculture exclusion zones
   e. wildflower and plant nature preserves

22. A possible result of overgrazing of grasslands is:
   a. deforestation
   b. soil saturation
   c. desertification
   d. increased protein production
   e. none of the above

23. The Sahel is a critical region that is located:
   a. in southern India
   b. in the Middle East
   c. just south of the Sahara Desert
   d. in southern Africa
   e. in the interior of Australia

24. Above all, most farmers rely on:
   a. climatic stability
   b. soil stability
   c. access to water
   d. temperature variation
   e. low labor costs

25. In von Thünen's isolated state model, the intensity of cultivation for any given crop increases as distance from the market increases.
   a. true
   b. false

PART TWO: Short answer (probable essay-type questions)

26. Briefly summarize the modified version of von Thünen's isolated state model.

_____

_____

_____

27. State the principle concepts and processes of aquaculture.

_____

_____

_____

28. Explain the difference between the American rectangular survey system and the "metes and bounds" survey system:

_____

_____

_____

29. What are the reasons for establishing "long-lot" farms and where can examples of these farms be found?

_____

_____

_____

30. What are GM crops and where are they most common? Why is this a problem for some?

_____

_____

_____

31. What does Professor Rod Neumann mean about "the importance of place in the global food system?"

_____

_____

_____

32. Explain and describe the highly distinctive type of subsistence agriculture called paddy rice farming.

_____

_____

_____

33. State some of the problems and benefits associated with the green revolution.

_____

_____

_____

34. Briefly describe the problems of commercial livestock fattening with regard to nutritional efficiency.

_____

_____

_____

35. What is the difference between a "suitcase farm" and agribusiness?

_____

_____

_____

36. What are the major world regions of commercial dairying?

_____

_____

_____

37. Describe the conditions and setting in which agriculture first arose.

_____

_____

_____

38. What are some of the major crops domesticated by the native peoples of the Americas?

_____

_____

_____

39. Briefly discuss the theme of cultural adaptation in agricultural geography.

_____

_____

_____

40. Briefly explain the pros and cons of biofuels.

_____

_____

_____

41. What are some examples of food fears?

_____

_____

_____

42. What is meant by "the global chicken"?

_____

_____

_____

43. What are some examples of indigenous technical knowledge?

_____

_____

_____

CHAPTER NINE

GEOGRAPHY OF ECONOMIES: INDUSTRIES, SERVICES, AND DEVELOPMENT

Extended Chapter Outline (Including Key Terms)

I. Regions
   A. Primary industry
   B. Secondary industry
   C. Services and information

II. Mobility of the Industrial Revolution
   A. Origins of the industrial revolution
   B. Diffusion from Britain
   C. Locational shifts
   D. Uneven development and deindustrialization
   E. Shifts of service industries

III. Economic Globalization
   A. Labor supply
   B. Markets
   C. Governments and globalization
   D. Globalization and cultural change

IV. Industrial Cultural Interaction
   A. Renewable resource crisis
   B. Acid rain
   C. Global climate change
      1. Ozone depletion
      2. Radioactive pollution
   D. Environmental sustainability

V. Cultural Landscapes
   A. Industrial landscapes
   B. Notebook: Imagining the New England Landscape

VI. Conclusion: Doing and Seeing Geography

LEARNING OBJECTIVES

After reading this chapter *and* studying the maps and illustrations, you should be able to:

1. Explain and define different categories of industry, including primary, secondary, and tertiary.

2. Trace the locations, origin, and diffusion of the industrial revolution.

3. Understand the strong effects of industrialization on the Earth's habitat and its people.

4. Explain the differences between ozone depletion, the greenhouse effect, and radioactive pollution, and describe the consequences of each.

5. Discuss the causal factors in the shifting locations of economic activity.

6. Identify elements of various industrial landscapes and the origins of these landscapes.

7. Contemplate the massive impact (evident today) of the industrial revolution on Earth, its people, its resources, and cultures.

SELECTED MAP READING AND INTERPRETATION

This section of the Study Guide is intended to increase your map-reading and interpretation skills. It will also help you apply the text readings to visual and spatial displays of concepts, themes, and examples in human and cultural geography.

A world atlas (in print or online) will be very useful in completing this section of the Study Guide and will enhance your comprehension of the maps in the textbook. Ask your instructor to recommend an appropriate website or atlas to purchase (or visit the map collection at your library). A world atlas is essential for your personal reference library, not only during this course, but throughout your college career.

After reading the text and studying the related map and its captions, answer the following questions.

FIGURE 9.1. World map of gross domestic product

1. Look at Europe. What do you think accounts for the east-west pattern of dollars per capita?

    _____
    _____
    _____

2. Does Africa show a north-south pattern of dollars per capita? Why or why not? What do you think are the reasons for these locational patterns?

    _____
    _____
    _____

3. Why do you think that "no data" exists for the countries of North Korea, Western Sahara, Somalia, Iraq, and Montenegro? Explain.

    _____
    _____
    _____

FIGURE 9.4. Major regions of industry in Anglo America

1. How would you delineate the major manufacturing belt in the United States and Canada?

    _____
    _____
    _____

2. Other than the major belt, which states share some of the minor regions

_____
_____
_____

FIGURE 9.5. *Industrial regions and deindustrialization in Europe*

1. If Western Europe is the wealthiest part of Europe, why has so much industrial decline taken place there?

   _____
   _____
   _____

2. Why are few luxury goods manufactured east of Germany and Italy? Is this situation changing?

   _____
   _____
   _____

3. Compare this map to a map showing the countries of the European Union. Do you see a relationship of any kind? Why or why not?

   _____
   _____
   _____

4. Explain the shifting locations of various industries in Europe.

   _____
   _____
   _____

FIGURE 9.12. *Global sites of export processing zones*

1. Explain the concentration of export processing zones along the U.S.–Mexico border and also in Central America.

   _____
   _____
   _____

2. What other major concentrations of export processing zones do you see and what do you think explains this pattern?

   _____
   _____
   _____

FIGURE 9.14. Tropical rain forest of the Amazon Basin

1. About 10,000 square miles of this rain forest are cleared each year. What are the reasons for this massive activity?

    _____

    _____

    _____

2. Can you identify any patterns on this map with regard to terrain or rivers? You will also need a physical map to answer this question.

    _____

    _____

    _____

FIGURE 9.16. Environmental Sustainability Index

1. Other than China, which countries rank lowest (worst) on this index?

    _____

    _____

    _____

2. Which countries rank highest (best) on this index? Why?

    _____

    _____

    _____

3. What global patterns does this map show? What can you infer from the patterns?

    _____

    _____

    _____

CREATE YOUR PERSONAL GLOSSARY OF KEY TERMS, PEOPLE, AND PLACES

In the space below, write a definition and provide an example of each key term that is sufficient for **your understanding**. It is an excellent study habit to organize your response in three parts:

1. A formal definition or identification from the textbook

2. A definition of the key term in **your own words**

3. An example to increase your understanding of the key term

KEY TERMS, PEOPLE, AND PLACES

1. Rostow's model

2. industrial revolution

3. primary industry

4. secondary industry

5. service industry

6. information industry

7. development

8. renewable resources

9. American Manufacturing Belt

10. economic core and periphery patterns

11. uneven development

12. technopoles

13. deindustrialization

14. global corporations

15. postindustrial phase

16. locational shifts

17. high-tech corridors

18. silicon landscapes

19. cottage industry

20. guild industry

21. fossil fuels

22. textiles

23. maquiladoras

24. mining

25. radioactive pollution

_____

_____

_____

26. Chernobyl

_____

_____

_____

27. acid rain

_____

_____

_____

28. greenhouse effect

_____

_____

_____

29. ozone layer

_____

_____

_____

30. ozone depletion

_____

_____

_____

31. labor-intensive industries

_____

_____

_____

32. ecotourism

_____

_____

_____

33. brownfields

_____

_____

_____

34. import-export tariffs and quotas

35. NAFTA and the EU

36. industrial landscape

37. Mona Domosh's Notebook

38. free trade

39. EPZs

40. Amazon Basin

41. global climate change

REVIEW: Self-Evaluation Tests

PART ONE: Multiple-choice

Circle the best answer for each question. When you are finished, read each question again with your selected answer. After you are satisfied with your practice test, use the Answer Key in the back of the Study Guide to check your responses.

1. The processing of raw materials into a more usable form is:
    a. primary industry
    b. secondary industry
    c. tertiary industry
    d. quaternary industry
    e. quinary industry

2. Agriculture is considered to be a:
    a. primary industry
    b. secondary industry
    c. tertiary industry
    d. quaternary industry
    e. quinary industry

3. The extraction of nonrenewable resources is a:
    a. primary industry
    b. secondary industry
    c. tertiary industry
    d. quaternary industry
    e. quinary industry

4. Legal services, retailing, and advertising are all considered:
    a. primary industry
    b. secondary industry
    c. tertiary industry
    d. quaternary industry
    e. quinary industry

5. Consumer-related services, such as education, are considered:
    a. primary industry
    b. secondary industry
    c. tertiary industry
    d. quaternary industry
    e. quinary industry

6. The American Manufacturing Belt is located:
    a. from Los Angeles to New York City
    b. primarily in the Lower South

   c. from Chicago to Pittsburgh
   d. around the Great Lakes and northeast states
   e. New England and the Piedmont

7. Multinational or transnational companies are also referred to as:
   a. global corporations
   b. international enterprises
   c. interregional industries
   d. global conglomerates
   e. none of the above

8. In Russia and the Ukraine, the most important mode of industrial transport is:
   a. highways
   b. railways
   c. airways
   d. waterways
   e. none of the above

9. While the cottage and guild industry systems were similar in many respects, only cottage industry depended on hand labor.
   a. true
   b. false

10. The initial breakthrough in the industrial revolution occurred in:
   a. the German steel industry
   b. the British smelting processes
   c. Dutch papermaking
   d. the British steel industry
   e. British textiles

11. The industrial revolution diffused from its place of origin first to:
   a. British colonies in North America
   b. British colonies in Africa and India
   c. continental Europe
   d. France
   e. the West Midlands of England

12. The worst area of acid rain pollution in the United States is/are:
   a. greater Los Angeles
   b. the Great Lakes states
   c. Texas and Louisiana
   d. the Great Plains
   e. none of the above

13. The basic cause of acid rain is the burning of:
    a. wood
    b. coal
    c. oil
    d. fossil fuels
    e. high-sulfur coal

14. Over 90 lakes are "dead" from acid rain in this seemingly pristine mountain range:
    a. the Adirondacks
    b. the Smoky Mountains
    c. the Catskills
    d. the Rockies
    e. the Canadian Rockies

15. Greenhouse effect is caused primarily by:
    a. burning coal
    b. burning fossil fuels
    c. ozone depletion
    d. the hole in the ozone layer
    e. none of the above

16. Carbon dioxide gases permit solar shortwave radiation to reach Earth's surface and allow outgoing long-wave radiation to escape.
    a. true
    b. false

17. Ozone-layer depletion is caused by:
    a. fossil fuels
    b. greenhouse effect
    c. global warming
    d. manufactured chemicals
    e. radioactive waste

18. A hotspot of ecotourism is/are:
    a. coral reef areas
    b. the Rocky Mountains
    c. the Great Lakes
    d. the Sahara Desert
    e. Arctic zones

19. In nearly all industrial site locations, a major factor is:
    a. the water supply
    b. politics
    c. the labor supply
    d. the electricity supply
    e. the climate

20. Coastal, often scenic, fishing villages from Norway to Portugal are part of the industrial landscape.
    a. true
    b. false

PART TWO: Short answer (probable essay-type questions)

21. What and where is the origin of the industrial revolution?

_____

_____

_____

22. What was the spatial and temporal pattern of industrial mobility and diffusion?

_____

_____

_____

23. What are primary industrial activities?

_____

_____

_____

24. What is the difference between service and information industrial activities?

_____

_____

_____

25. Where is most secondary industrial activity located in North America?

_____

_____

_____

26. What was the diffusion pattern of the industrial revolution in Europe?

_____

_____

_____

27. Why did the highway displace the railroad in America as a major factor with regard to industry?

_____

_____

_____

28. What are the sources of radioactive pollution?

_____

_____

_____

29. How is acid rain created and which regions does it strongly affect?

_____

_____

_____

30. What are the major problems associated with dependence on fossil fuels?

_____

_____

_____

31. What are the main differences between the greenhouse effect, ozone depletion, and global warming?

_____

_____

_____

32. Explain the causal factors of the greenhouse effect.

_____

_____

_____

33. What is meant by the "environmental" reaction?

_____

_____

_____

34. Describe the New England landscape as "imagined" by Mona Domosh.

_____

_____

_____

35. Describe some environmental factors in industrial location.

_____

_____

_____

36. Describe the various relationships between labor and industrial location:

_____

_____

_____

37. What all-encompassing cultural changes were brought about by the industrial revolution?

_____

_____

_____

38. Explain the various impacts politics can have on industry.

_____

_____

_____

39. Describe the types of industrial landscapes that result from primary, secondary, and quaternary industries.

_____

_____

_____

40. Provide examples of how the industrial landscape is interpreted by some humanists.

_____

_____

_____

41. How does international tourism impact economics and cultures globally and locally?

_____

_____

_____

42. What is ecotourism and where is it usually practiced? By whom?

_____

_____

_____

CHAPTER TEN

URBANIZATION: THE CITY IN TIME AND SPACE

Extended Chapter Outline (including Key Terms)

I. Urban Region
    A. Patterns and processes
    B. Impacts
    C. Central-place theory

II. Mobility
    A. Origin and diffusion of the city
    B. Models for the rise of cities
    C. Urban hearth areas
    D. Diffusion of the city from hearth areas
    E. Rural-to-urban migration

III. Globalization
    A. Global cities
    B. Globalizing cities

IV. Nature-Culture and Cities
    A. Site and situation
    B. Defensive sites
    C. Trade-route sites
    D. Urbanization and sustainability
    E. Natural disasters

V. Cultural Landscape and Urban Geography
    A. Globalizing cities in the developing world
        1. Squatter settlements
        2. EMRs (extended metropolitan regions)
    B. Latin American cities
    C. Apartheid and the postapartheid city
    D. Socialist and postsocialist cities

VI. Conclusion

LEARNING OBJECTIVES

After reading this chapter *and* studying the maps and illustrations, you should be able to:

1. Define the term "city" and discuss the meaning of "urbanized population."

2. Explain various theories dealing with the origin and diffusion of the city.

3. Demonstrate knowledge of urban hearth areas and the 10 largest urban centers today.

4. Discuss the evolution of urban landscapes.

5. Understand the problems of the globalized city.

6. Explain the causal factors that led to the capitalist city.

7. Discuss the impact of industrialization on city structure.

8. Understand various models of cities in developing countries.

9. Describe Latin American, postapartheid, and postsocialist cities.

10. Interpret with new understanding various cities with which you are familiar.

SELECTED MAP READING AND INTERPRETATION

This section of the Study Guide is intended to increase your map-reading and interpretation skills. It will also help you apply the text readings to visual and spatial displays of concepts, themes, and examples in human and cultural geography.

A world atlas (in print or online) will be very useful in completing this section of the Study Guide and will enhance your comprehension of the maps in the textbook. Ask your instructor to recommend an appropriate web site or atlas to purchase (or visit the map collection at your library). A world atlas is essential for your personal reference library, not only during this course, but throughout your college career.

After reading the text and studying the related map and its captions, answer the following questions.

FIGURE 10.1. Urbanized population in the world

1. Although China and India have more people than any other countries, what accounts for their relatively low amount of urbanization?

   _____

   _____

   _____

2. Can you think of environmental factors for the high percentage of urbanization in such countries as Australia, Saudi Arabia, and Libya? What do these countries have in common?

   _____

   _____

   _____

3. Speculate on the reasons behind the apparent difference between the Eastern and Western Hemispheres in term of urbanized population.

   _____

   _____

   _____

FIGURE 10.5. The world's first cities arose in six urban hearth areas

1. In which countries are these ancient hearth areas, such as Mesopotamia, located today?

   _____

   _____

   _____

2. What are the major rivers associated, if any, with each of these specific hearth areas?

_____

_____

_____

FIGURE 10.17. *Large cities in relation to current climate-related hazards*

1. Where are the highest-risk cities located in North America?

_____

_____

_____

2. Is there a correlation shown between high-risk-hazard areas and urbanization? Why or why not?

_____

_____

_____

3. What global patterns can you identify here? Do you see a pattern of physical environments or terrain related to hazard areas?

_____

_____

_____

FIGURE 10.19. *Diagram of Hanoi's extended metropolitan region*

1. Compare this city to an American city. How and why is it different?

_____

_____

_____

2. What are the site and situation of Hanoi?

_____

_____

_____

CREATE YOUR PERSONAL GLOSSARY OF KEY TERMS, PEOPLE, AND PLACES

In the space below, write a definition and provide an example of each key term that is sufficient for **your understanding**. It is an excellent study habit to organize your response in three parts:

1. A formal definition or identification from the textbook

2. A definition of the key term in **your own words**

3. An example to increase your understanding of the key term

KEY TERMS, PEOPLE, AND PLACES

1. urbanized population

_____
_____
_____

2. rural-to-urban migration

_____
_____
_____

3. the world's 10 largest metropolitan areas

_____
_____
_____

4. primate city

_____
_____
_____

5. city model

_____
_____
_____

6. hydraulic civilization

_____
_____
_____

7. global city

8. multiple-factor models

9. urban hearth areas

10. axis mundi

11. squatter settlements

12. urban morphology

13. zoning

14. institution of kingship

15. Kris Olds

16. Roman Empire

_____
_____
_____

17. defensive sites

_____
_____
_____

18. the medieval period

_____
_____
_____

19. river-island site

_____
_____
_____

20. Hurricane Katrina

_____
_____
_____

21. barriadas

_____
_____
_____

22. New Orleans

_____
_____
_____

23. urbanization and sustainability

_____
_____
_____

24. EMRs

_____
_____
_____

25. apartheid and city structure

26. the capitalist city

27. industrial city

28. postsocialist city

29. benefits of agglomeration

30. megacities

31. central-place theory

32. rural

33. Christaller

34. colonial city

_____
_____
_____

35. gridiron street pattern

_____
_____
_____

36. agricultural surplus

_____
_____
_____

37. Mesopotamia

_____
_____
_____

38. "site" and "situation"

_____
_____
_____

39. Indus Valley

_____
_____
_____

40. acropolis sites

_____
_____
_____

41. trade-route sites

_____
_____
_____

42. spatial distribution of cities

_____
_____
_____

43. Mesoamerica

_____

_____

_____

44. cosmomagical cities

_____

_____

_____

REVIEW: Self-Evaluation Tests

PART ONE: Multiple-choice

Circle the best answer for each question. When you are finished, read each question again with your selected answer. After you are satisfied with your practice test, use the Answer Key in the back of the Study Guide to check your responses.

1. "Urbanized population" refers to a country's:
   a. number of cities
   b. number of cities over 100,000 in population
   c. percentage of urban population
   d. ratio of urban to rural population
   e. none of the above

2. The U.S. Census Bureau defines a city as a densely populated area of _____ people or more.
   a. 2500
   b. 5000
   c. 10,000
   d. 20,000
   e. 50,000

3. The term "global cities" refers to cities that have populations of at least:
   a. 500,000
   b. 1,000,000
   c. 5,000,000
   d. 10,000,000
   e. none of the above

4. Which of the following cities is NOT ranked in the world's 10 largest metropolitan areas?
   a. Seoul
   b. London
   c. Moscow
   d. New York
   e. Bombay

5. The city that dominates the political, economic, and cultural life of a country is the _____ city.
   a. capital
   b. most populous
   c. vanguard
   d. primate
   e. growth pole

6. The origin of cities is strongly related to:
   a. plant and animal domestication
   b. improved transportation networks
   c. warfare and defense
   d. improved building techniques
   e. all of the above

7. The hydraulic civilization model can be tied to all of the following urban hearths
   except:
   a. China
   b. Mesoamerica
   c. Egypt
   d. Mesopotamia (Iraq)
   e. Indus River valley

8. Cosmomagical cities exhibit these three spatial characteristics: a
   _____, a symbolic center, and a cardinal direction orientation.
   a. walled circumference
   b. walled outer city
   c. universe-like form
   d. wheel spoke form
   e. moat or bulwark

9. The pattern of functional land use within a city is referred to as:
   a. urban morphology
   b. functional development
   c. functional zonation
   d. spatial landscapes
   e. urban land use

10. The place for public use and markets in ancient Greek cities was the:
    a. agora
    b. citadel
    c. forum
    d. acropolis
    e. castra

11. The _____ was the urban zone of a Roman city where religious, administrative,
    and educational structures, as well as markets, were located.
    a. agora
    b. citadel
    c. forum
    d. acropolis
    e. castra

12. The most important contribution or legacy of Roman city builders was probably:
    a. engineering
    b. transportation
    c. architecture
    d. site selection
    e. gridiron planning

13. Globalizing cities are strongly associated with:
    a. migration
    b. postindustrialism
    c. geopolitics
    d. religion, especially Islam
    e. the automotive industry

14. The medieval town's crowning glory was usually the:
    a. town hall
    b. castle
    c. fortress
    d. cathedral
    e. clock tower

15. The term and concept of central-place was created by:
    a. Walter Christaller
    b. Walter Kollmorgen
    c. Lewis Mumford
    d. Alfred Weber
    e. Jean Gottmann

16. A majority of the American people were not urbanized until:
    a. 1890
    b. 1920
    c. 1940
    d. 1950
    e. 1960

17. The regional setting of an urban location is called the:
    a. site
    b. node
    c. ecological niche
    d. situation
    e. none of the above

18. Mexico City, Montreal, New York City, and Venice are all examples of:
    a. limited access cities
    b. colonial cities
    c. river-island sites

d. acropolis sites

e. defensive sites

19. Critical to central-place theory is the fact that different goods and services vary both in _____ and range.

a. spatial distribution

b. quality

c. quantity

d. threshold

e. access

20. An "edge city" is any place that has the following features, except:

a. 1 million square feet or less of leasable office space

b. 600,000 square feet or more of leasable retail space

c. more jobs than bedrooms

d. it is perceived by people as one place

e. it was not at all urban as recently as 30 years ago

21. Large-scale squatter settlements are a typical feature of many:

a. Mexican cities

b. European and Russian cities

c. "developing" world cities

d. former French and Portuguese colonies

e. North African and Middle Eastern cities

22. Mona's notebook explored urbanization while finding a FedEx office in the city of:

a. Budapest

b. Warsaw

c. Prague

d. Vienna

e. Berlin

PART TWO: Short answer (probable essay-type questions)

23. Briefly explain "threshold" and "range" in central-place theory.

_____

_____

_____

24. What did Christaller add to central-place theory in his second model?

_____

_____

_____

25. List some common features of former colonial cities.

_____

_____

_____

26. What are some of the major problems faced by cities in Africa, Mesoamerica, and India?

_____

_____

_____

27. Describe a squatter settlement, and include a couple of actual examples.

_____

_____

_____

28. Clearly explain the difference between site and situation.

_____

_____

_____

29. What are characteristics of the postsocialist city?

_____

_____

_____

30. What is meant by megacity?

_____

_____

_____

31. What role does "race" play in urban function and features?

_____

_____

_____

32. Describe some main features of the institution of kingship.

_____

_____

_____

33. What are the spatial features associated with cosmomagical cities?

_____

_____

_____

34. Discuss an argument concerning the diffusion of the city from hearth areas.

_____

_____

_____

35. What are characteristics of the postapartheid city?

_____

_____

_____

36. What are characteristics of the Latin American city?

_____

_____

_____

37. Prague's central city did not develop as a financial center of high-rise office buildings, unlike many other cities of Central and Western Europe. Explain why this happened.

_____

_____

_____

CHAPTER ELEVEN

INSIDE THE CITY: A CULTURAL MOSAIC

Extended Chapter Outline (Including Key Terms)

I. Urban Culture Regions
   A. Downtowns
   B. Residential
   C. Homelessness
   D. Models of U.S. and Canadian cities
      1. Concentric zone model
      2. Sector model
      3. Multiple nuclei model

II. Mobility and the City
   A. Centralization
   B. Suburbanization and decentralization
      1. Economic and social advantages
      2. Public policy
   C. The costs of decentralization
   D. Gentrification

III. Globalization and the City
   A. New ethnic neighborhoods
   B. Global urban form?

IV. Nature-Culture
   A. Urban weather and climate
   B. Urban hydrology
   C. Urban vegetation

V. Cultural Landscapes
   A. Themes in cityscape study
      1. Landscape dynamics
      2. The city as palimpsest
      3. Symbolic cityscapes
      4. Perception of the city
   B. Landscape histories of American, Canadian, and European cities
      1. Greek cities
      2. Roman cities
      3. Medieval cities
      4. Renaissance and Baroque periods

LEARNING OBJECTIVES

After reading this chapter *and* studying the maps and illustrations, you should be able to:

1. Identify and describe various and distinct city culture regions.

2. Understand the concept, views, perception, and importance of the "neighborhood" and its role in everyday life.

3. Explain the difference between and the pros and cons of centralization and decentralization of the city.

4. Understand the elements of the urban ecosystem and its impact on society.

5. Identify various city models and relate them to actual cities.

6. Understand the elements of the city landscape and its causal factors.

7. Identify symbolic, cultural, and perceptive elements of the city environment.

8. Trace the history of the basic city landscape in Europe and North America.

9. Understand the role of globalization in city life, as well as the dynamics of city life.

10. Begin to look at and interpret, with new awareness, the cities and neighborhoods around you.

SELECTED MAP READING AND INTERPRETATION

This section of the Study Guide is intended to increase your map-reading and interpretation skills. It will also help you apply the text readings to visual and spatial displays of concepts, themes, and examples in human and cultural geography.

A world atlas (in print or online) will be very useful in completing this section of the Study Guide and will enhance your comprehension of the maps in the textbook. Ask your instructor to recommend an appropriate website or atlas to purchase (or visit the map collection at your library). A world atlas is essential for your personal reference library, not only during this course, but throughout your college career.

After reading the text and studying the related map and its captions, answer the following questions.

FIGURE 11.16. Map indicating the location of 10 metropolitan areas in the United States

1. Why is immigration focused on these specific cities?

   _____

   _____

   _____

2. Why do you think that some major cities, such as Detroit, Seattle, Denver, Cleveland, and Phoenix, are not included in these statistics?

   _____

   _____

   _____

FIGURE 11.28. Diffusion of urbanization in Europe.

1. Explain this pattern of diffusion.

   _____

   _____

   _____

2. This map shows that it took 1000 years for urbanization to spread from northern Italy to northern England. Why do you think it was so slow? What were the barriers to diffusion?

   _____

   _____

   _____

3. Compare this to a current map of Europe and find major cities in each region that illustrate the path of diffusion.

   _____

   _____

   _____

CREATE YOUR PERSONAL GLOSSARY OF KEY TERMS, PEOPLE, AND PLACES

In the space below, write a definition and provide an example of each key term that is sufficient for **your understanding**. It is an excellent study habit to organize your response in three parts:

1. A formal definition or identification from the textbook

2. A definition of the key term in **your own words**

3. An example to increase your understanding of the key term

KEY TERMS, PEOPLE, AND PLACES

1. social culture region

2. ethnic culture region

3. census tracts

4. neighborhood

5. definitions of homelessness

6. "zone in transition"

7. centralizing forces

8. decentralizing forces

_____
_____
_____

9. economic and social advantages of centralization

_____
_____
_____

10. agglomeration or clustering

_____
_____
_____

11. "streetcar suburbs"

_____
_____
_____

12. decentralization

_____
_____
_____

13. economic and social advantages of decentralization

_____
_____
_____

14. lateral commuting

_____
_____
_____

15. Federal Housing Administration

_____
_____
_____

16. covenants

_____
_____
_____

17. redlining

18. costs of decentralization

19. gentrification

20. sexuality and gentrification

21. costs of gentrification

22. urban ecology

23. urban geology

24. urban heat island

25. urban hydrology

26. runoff

_____
_____
_____

27. urban vegetation

_____
_____
_____

28. segregation

_____
_____
_____

29. new ethnic neighborhoods

_____
_____
_____

30. concentric zone model

_____
_____
_____

31. CBD

_____
_____
_____

32. sector model

_____
_____
_____

33. Homer Hoyt

_____
_____
_____

34. Ernest Burgess

_____
_____
_____

35. multiple-nuclei models

_____
_____
_____

36. feminist critique

_____
_____
_____

37. Latin American model

_____
_____
_____

38. spine/sector

_____
_____
_____

39. Mona's Notebook: "Seeing New Places"

_____
_____
_____

40. Greek cities

_____
_____
_____

41. Roman city planning

_____
_____
_____

42. urban landscape and cityscape

_____
_____
_____

43. medieval city: charter, wall, marketplace, cathedral

_____
_____
_____

44. city as palimpsest

_____
_____
_____

45. symbolic cityscape

_____
_____
_____

46. ghetto

_____
_____
_____

47. perception of the city

_____
_____
_____

48. Renaissance and Baroque periods

_____
_____
_____

49. office parks

_____
_____
_____

50. high-tech corridors

_____
_____
_____

51. festival settings

_____
_____
_____

52. militarized space

_____
_____
_____

53. public space

_____
_____
_____

REVIEW: Self-Evaluation Tests

PART ONE: Multiple-choice

Circle the best answer for each question. When you are finished, read each question again with your selected answer. After you are satisfied with your practice test, use the Answer Key in the back of the Study Guide to check your responses.

1. An excellent way to define social regions is to isolate one social trait and plot its distribution within a city by using:
   a. aerial maps
   b. satellite imagery
   c. census tracts
   d. telephone directories
   e. property tax records

2. The neighborhood concept is critical to cultural geography because it:
   a. recognizes the sentiment people have for places
   b. provides examples of race relations within cities
   c. illustrates and explores urban ecology
   d. helps us understand spatial structures of cities
   e. none of the above

3. An important economic advantage to central city location has traditionally been:
   a. product cost
   b. advertising
   c. proximity to major transport networks
   d. accessibility
   e. all of the above

4. Agglomeration or clustering is considered:
   a. an economic disadvantage
   b. an economic advantage
   c. the hope for the future of neighborhoods
   d. an out-of-date method of urban planning
   e. only used in North American cities

5. Today, many people travel to work from suburb to suburb. This is called:
   a. suburban dependency
   b. bypass commuting
   c. lateral commuting
   d. highway bypass commuting
   e. none of the above

6. "FHA" is the abbreviation for which government body or legislation?
   a. the Fair Housing Act
   b. the Federal Home Association
   c. the Family Housing Act

d. the Federal Housing Act

e. the Federal Housing Administration

7. A practice in which banks and mortgage companies designate areas as high risk for loans is:

a. redistricting

b. redlining

c. covenants

d. blacklisting

e. none of the above

8. The movement of middle-class people into deteriorated areas of a city center is referred to as:

a. urban revitalization

b. urban renewal

c. gentrification

d. insanity

e. reverse out-migration

9. Lower-income people of the inner city are often displaced by the process of:

a. urban sprawl

b. urban housing projects

c. gentrification

d. homelessness

e. reverse out-migration

10. The study of the relationship between an organism and its physical environment is called:

a. physical geography

b. physical geology

c. earth science

d. ecology

e. cultural ecology

11. The direction of city growth, the patterning of social regions, and the routing of transportation can all be influenced by:

a. topography

b. river and waterway patterns

c. climate

d. seasonality

e. temperature variation

12. The heat generated by a city produces a large mass of warmer air sitting over the city called an urban heat island.

a. true

b. false

13. During the summer, a city center is warmer than its suburbs.
    a. true
    b. false

14. The concentric zone model of Burgess has five zones. Zone 2, characterized by a mixed pattern of industrial and residential land use, is considered a _____ zone.
    a. stable
    b. blue-collar
    c. transitional
    d. better housing
    e. gentrified

15. The area of the concentric zone model characterized by commuters and high-income families is zone _____.
    a. 1
    b. 2
    c. 3
    d. 4
    e. 5

16. The sector model of urban land use was developed by:
    a. Burgess
    b. Hoyt
    c. Harris
    d. Ullman
    e. none of the above

17. Freeways became part of the city landscape:
    a. after 1945
    b. before 1940
    c. in the 1950s
    d. in the 1960s
    e. before 1930

18. The model that maintains that a city develops with equal intensity around various points is the _____ model.
    a. sector
    b. concentric zone
    c. urban growth
    d. multiple nuclei
    e. none of the above

19. You have been given an assignment based on a census tract where you live. Using 1950 and 2000 census data, you are to map and analyze changes in population numbers, age structure, and education and income levels. Which of the following statements is NOT correct concerning this assignment?
    a. You will be mapping formal regions.
    b. The stated criteria define social culture regions.

c. Your maps might include ethnic culture neighborhoods.

d. Your results are likely to have very clearly demarcated lines with no overlap between social culture regions and ethnic culture regions.

e. All of the above statements are correct.

20. A palimpsest is a:
   a. section of most American cities
   b. section of most European cities
   c. critical part of the sector model
   d. reference to transport planning
   e. parchment used over and over for written messages

21. A cemetery may be considered part of a city's:
   a. park system
   b. symbolic landscape
   c. palimpsest
   d. CBD
   e. all of the above

22. Which of the following is considered a "landmark"?
   a. city hall
   b. a railway depot
   c. an industrial smokestack
   d. White Castle restaurant
   e. all of the above

23. Shopping malls in North America are _____ spaces.
   a. eternal
   b. urban
   c. private
   d. open
   e. public

24. Major cities of medieval Europe had all of the following except:
   a. city walls
   b. estate manor houses
   c. cathedrals
   d. charters
   e. marketplaces or squares

25. Many U.S. cities have a pattern of leapfrog expansion, and then in-filling, to use all of the space inside the city limits.
   a. true
   b. false

PART TWO: Short answer (probable essay-type questions)

26. What human factors define a neighborhood?

_____

_____

_____

27. What is meant by the "city as palimpsest"?

_____

_____

_____

28. Describe elements of a neighborhood that you are familiar with.

_____

_____

_____

29. What are the characteristics of the Latin American model zones?

_____

_____

_____

30. What are the elements of Homer Hoyt's urban model?

_____

_____

_____

31. How is the focus of this chapter different from that of Chapter 10?

_____

_____

_____

32. List some symbols and landmarks of the urban environment.

_____

_____

_____

33. How do cities affect the natural environment and ecology?

_____

_____

_____

34. What does Mona Domosh say about "seeing" new places?

_____

_____

_____

35. What are some criticisms of the concentric zone model?

_____

_____

_____

36. What is the feminist critique in urban geography?

_____

_____

_____

37. Briefly discuss the role of race and gender in the urban mosaic.

_____

_____

_____

38. Describe the concept of the shopping mall as a social center.

_____

_____

_____

39. What are some of the costs of city decentralization?

_____

_____

_____

40. How did the streetcar and trolley affect neighborhood development in the late nineteenth and early twentieth centuries?

_____

_____

_____

41. Are neighborhoods found in the suburbs? Why or why not?

_____

_____

_____

42. What are some of the human costs of gentrification?

_____

_____

_____

43. How does topography influence city growth and structure?

_____

_____

_____

44. Is urban hydrology a factor in the future of cities? How and why?

_____
_____
_____

45. What are the problems of defining "homelessness"?

_____
_____
_____

46. Describe the composition of the new ethnic neighborhoods.

_____
_____
_____

47. What are some patterns of new ethnic migration and city destinations in North America?

_____
_____
_____

48. How did the Greeks build cities and what are these cities' key features.

_____
_____
_____

49. Describe Roman city planning.

_____
_____
_____

50. What are the basic elements of the European medieval city?

_____
_____
_____

CHAPTER TWELVE

ONE WORLD OR MANY? THE CULTURAL GEOGRAPHY OF THE FUTURE

Extended Chapter Outline

I. Regions of the Future
    A. Uneven geography
    B. One Europe or many?
    C. Glocalization
    D. Geography of the Internet

II. Mobility
    A. Information superhighway
    B. New (auto) mobilities
    C. Global tourists

III. Globalization
    A. Deeper look
    B. History, geography, and globalization
    C. Globalization and its discontents
    D. Blending sounds

IV. Nature-Culture
    A. Sustainability
    B. Think globally, act locally

V. Cultural Landscape
    A. Globalized
    B. Striving for the unique
    C. Wal-Martians invade!
    D. Europe's rural landscape

VIII. Conclusion

SELECTED MAP READING AND INTERPRETATION

This section of the Study Guide is intended to increase your map-reading and interpretation skills. It will also help you apply the text readings to visual and spatial displays of concepts, themes, and examples in human and cultural geography.

A world atlas (in print or online) will be very useful in completing this section of the Study Guide and will enhance your comprehension of the maps in the textbook. Ask your instructor to recommend an appropriate website or atlas to purchase (or visit the map collection at your library). A world atlas is essential for your personal reference library, not only during this course, but throughout your college career.

After reading the text and studying the related map and its captions, answer the following questions.

FIGURE 12.3. Map of government filtering practices show that nation-state boundaries...

1. Recent events involve many people in the Arab countries of the Middle East and North Africa rising up against their often oppressive government. Identify Arab-speaking countries on this map and indicate their level of filtering:

   _____
   _____
   _____

2. Based on your knowledge of world affairs, do you find the various government filtering activities here predictable or surprising?

   _____
   _____
   _____

3. Which countries of Asia show no evidence or no data regarding filtering?

   _____
   _____
   _____

FIGURE 12.4. Connections to the Internet

1. In which regions of Earth do you find relatively low frequency of Internet connections? How can this affect a country's economic and cultural future?

   _____
   _____
   _____

2. Can you think of any locational incentives for Australia, New Zealand, and Scandinavia to have very high frequency of Internet connections?

_____

_____

_____

FIGURE 12.5. Diffusion of the Internet

1. Compare this map with Figure 12.4. Do the countries with the earliest Internet connections have the highest frequency of connections now? Does India? Why or why not?

_____

_____

_____

2. What are the reasons for these patterns of diffusion? Economic, political, technical? Explain.

_____

_____

_____

Lessons and Purpose of Chapter Twelve

This chapter is somewhat different from the previous sections of your text. It is a chapter about the geography of the future. *We are all interested in the future because that is where we will spend the rest of our lives.*

In lieu of multiple-choice practice tests and key terms, the following section of major essay questions is provided for your thoughts and notes.

1. What is meant by the "end of geography" in relation to globalization? What will be the landscapes of the future?

———————————————————————————
———————————————————————————
———————————————————————————
———————————————————————————
———————————————————————————
———————————————————————————
———————————————————————————
———————————————————————————
———————————————————————————
———————————————————————————
———————————————————————————
———————————————————————————
———————————————————————————
———————————————————————————
———————————————————————————
———————————————————————————
———————————————————————————
———————————————————————————
———————————————————————————
———————————————————————————
———————————————————————————
———————————————————————————
———————————————————————————
———————————————————————————
———————————————————————————
———————————————————————————
———————————————————————————

2. Describe various critiques and actions, both pro and con, regarding globalization:

_____
_____
_____
_____
_____
_____
_____
_____
_____
_____
_____
_____
_____
_____
_____
_____
_____
_____
_____
_____

3. Discuss how media and the Internet will (or do) challenge and change geography:

_____
_____
_____
_____
_____
_____
_____
_____
_____
_____
_____
_____
_____
_____
_____
_____
_____
_____
_____

4. Is sustainability the key to future development of the people of the world? Must this be done in a "green" frame of mind and action?

_____
_____
_____
_____
_____

5. Describe the United States or Canada, 30 years into the future. Include ethnicity, transportation, energy, housing, culture, race, economy, and cities in your proposed view of the 2040s decade.

MULTIPLE-CHOICE ANSWER SECTION

CHAPTER ONE ANSWER KEY

1. c   2. b   3. d   4. c   5. b   6. b   7. b   8. b   9. d   10. e   11. c

12. a   13. a   14. c   15. c   16. d   17. b   18. c   19. a   20. d   21. b   22. c

23. d   24. a   25. c

CHAPTER TWO ANSWER KEY

1. c   2. a   3. d   4. b   5. d   6. b   7. c   8. c   9. a   10. a   11. d

12. d   13. c   14. d   15. d   16. b   17. b   18. d   19. c   20. a   21. d   22. d

23. a   24. a   25. d   26. d   27. c   28. d   29. a   30. b   31. a   32. b   33. d

34. d   35. a   36. c

CHAPTER THREE ANSWER KEY

1. d   2. c   3. b   4. a   5. c   6. a   7. b   8. a   9. d   10. c   11. d

12. c or d   13. a   14. a   15. b   16. b   17. b   18. c   19. d   20. d   21. b

22. b   23. a

CHAPTER FOUR ANSWER KEY

1. d   2. d   3. c   4. b   5. a   6. d   7. d   8. b   9. a   10. a   11. d

12. b   13. c   14. c   15. d   16. c   17. d   18. a   19. d   20. d   21. b   22. a

CHAPTER FIVE ANSWER KEY

1. c   2. b   3. a   4. d   5. d   6. a   7. b   8. c   9. c   10. c   11. a

12. b   13. c   14. b   15. a   16. c   17. c   18. d   19. c   20. a   21. a   22. d   23. c

CHAPTER SIX ANSWER KEY

1. d   2. a   3. c   4. b   5. d   6. b   7. b   8. d   9. b   10. b   11. c

12. d   13. a   14. b   15. d   16. a   17. a   18. d   19. c   20. d   21. b   22. d

23. d   24. d   25. d   26. b   27. c   28. d

CHAPTER SEVEN ANSWER KEY

1. b   2. c   3. d   4. d   5. c   6. a   7. d   8. d   9. d   10. b   11. a

12. d   13. d   14. d   15. b   16. b   17. c   18. a   19. b   20. a   21. a   22. c

23. a   24. c   25. d   26. c

CHAPTER EIGHT ANSWER KEY

1. d   2. a   3. b   4. d   5. c   6. b   7. a   8. d   9. c   10. d   11. a

12. c   13. d   14. b   15. d   16. d   17. b   18. b   19. c   20. a   21. c   22. c

23. c   24. a   25. b

CHAPTER NINE ANSWER KEY

1. b   2. a   3. a   4. c   5. d   6. d   7. b   8. b   9. b   10. d   11. c

12. b   13. d   14. a   15. b   16. b   17. d   18. a   19. a   20. a

CHAPTER TEN ANSWER KEY

1. c 2. a 3. d 4. b or c 5. d 6. a 7. b 8. c 9. c 10. a

11. c 12. d 13. a 14. d 15. a 16. b 17. d 18. c 19. d 20. a 21. c 22. c

CHAPTER ELEVEN ANSWER KEY

1. c 2. d 3. d 4. b 5. c 6. d 7. b 8. c 9. c 10. d 11. a

12. a 13. a 14. c 15. d 16. b 17. a 18. d 19. d 20. d 21. b 22. d 23. c

24. b 25. a

NOTES